GETTING A GRIP
ON THE BASICS OF
PRAYER

GETTING A GRIP ON THE BASICS
BIBLE STUDY SERIES

bethjones

All Scripture quotations, unless otherwise indicated, are from the New King James Version®. Copyright © 1982, Thomas Nelson, Inc. All rights reserved. Bible text from the New King James Version® is not to be reproduced in copies or otherwise by any means except as permitted in writing by Thomas Nelson, Inc., Attn: Bible Rights and Permissions, PO Box 141000, Nashville, TN 37214-1000.

Scripture quotations marked AMPC are taken from the Amplified Bible, Copyright © 1954, 1958, 1962, 1964, 1965, 1987 by The Lockman Foundation. Used by permission.

Scriptures marked KJV are taken from the KING JAMES VERSION: KING JAMES VERSION, public domain.

Scriptures marked NASB are from the New American Standard Bible®. Copyright © 1960, 1962, 1963, 1971, 1972, 1973, 1975, 1977, 1995 by The Lockman Foundation. Used by permission. All rights reserved.

Scriptures marked NCV are taken from the New Century Version®. Copyright © 2005 by Thomas Nelson. Used by permission. All rights reserved.

Scriptures marked NLT are from the Holy Bible, New Living Translation, Copyright © 1996. Used by permission of Tyndale House Publishers, Inc., Wheaton, Illinois 60189. All rights reserved.

Scripture quotations marked TPT are from The Passion Translation®. Copyright © 2017, 2018, 2020 by Passion & Fire Ministries, Inc. Used by permission. All rights reserved. ThePassionTranslation.com.

Scripture quotations marked YLT are taken from the 1898 YOUNG'S LITERAL TRANSLATION OF THE HOLY BIBLE by J.N. Young, (Author of the Young's Analytical Concordance), public domain.

Published by Harrison House Publishers
Shippensburg, PA 17257

ISBN 13 TP: 978-1-6803-1795-4
ISBN 13 eBook: 978-1-6803-1796-1

Jeff and Beth Jones Ministries
Portage, Michigan
the basicswithbeth.com

For Worldwide Distribution, Printed in the U.S.A.
1 2 3 4 5 6 7 8 / 25 24 23 22 21

TABLE OF CONTENTS

SECTION 4: THE "WHY" OF PRAYER

SECTION 5: THE "HOW" OF PRAYER

SECTION 6: THE "WHEN" OF PRAYER

SECTION 7: THE "WHERE" OF PRAYER

SECTION 1:

THE "WHO, WHAT, WHEN, WHERE, WHY, AND HOW" OF PRAYER

CHAPTER 1:

PRAYER BASICS

"The man who mobilizes the Christian Church to pray
will make the greatest contribution to world evangelism in history."
Andrew Murray

What if you were offered a key that opened the door to a special room where you could *visit* with the most loving and powerful Person in all the universe. *Would you take it?* What if you were *given* a treasure map and the chance to go on a lifetime adventure to access the most incredible stash of blessings, wisdom, revelation, power and miracles—plus everything else you need. *Would you follow it?* What if you were *invited* to play an important role on a high-level strategic team that would affect the world and influence eternity. *Would you accept it?*

You have *already* been given all those things through the power and privilege of prayer!

>> Through prayer, you get to *visit* with your heavenly Father, your Lord Jesus, and the Holy Spirit in the most intimate ways as you spend time together (Psalm 27:4).

>> Through prayer, you have been *given* everything you need to request every spiritual blessing reserved for you in heavenly places (Ephesians 1:3).

>> Through prayer, you are *invited* to partner with God to establish His will "on earth as it is in heaven" (Matthew 6:10).

Does this excite you? It should!

I'll be honest, in my own life, when I think about the most exciting and significant experiences I have had with the Lord and the most important events and seasons in my life and ministry, they are all deeply connected to intentional prayer. I can't imagine being a Christian without the ability to express my heart in prayer to the Lord, or without the opportunity to request the things I need, or without the chance to go on a prayer-filled, faith adventure with God to do kingdom business. (I wouldn't want to imagine it!)

Prayer is our connection to God. Without prayer, the Christian life would just be an accumulation of knowledge and theory. That's why I am so excited about taking you on this prayer journey.

A. HARDWIRED TO PRAY

We are hardwired to pray. It seems that people throughout history, from all religions, nations, tribes, and tongues have an innate reflex to pray. The desire to pray appears to be built into our spiritual DNA. At our core, talking to and hearing from our creator is the cry of every human heart.

When I reflect on the various places around the world that my husband and I have been fortunate enough to visit, at the top of the list are well-known places of prayer: the Wailing Wall and the Upper Room in Jerusalem, the Temple of the Emerald Buddha in Thailand, the Blue Mosque in Istanbul, Vatican City and St. Peter's Basilica outside of Rome, and the many temple ruins in Athens, Corinth, Ephesus, and throughout Greece.

In these places and thousands more, Christians and non-Christians alike have stood, knelt, marched, wailed, cried, and prayed. As I have stood in the places mentioned and watched people of all faiths pray, I have had a mix of emotions. Many times my heart has been happy to see so many people hungry for a God they know exists.

At the same time, I have felt grieved, heavy, and sad. It's grievous to see people desperately rocking back and forth, wailing and begging their god to do something. It's heart-wrenching to see others curled up for hours counting their prayer beads with the hope they've offered enough prayer to get an answer. It is distressing to watch people throw the little bit of money they have at a man-made idol with the hopes of answered prayers. It's troubling to hear people pray from a place of fear and doubt rather than gratitude and faith.

Perhaps, the most heartbreaking thing about the kinds of prayers we've mentioned is the disappointment sincere people face from the lack of answers they receive and their resulting frustration—and worse, they blame God. How must God's heart grieve over all of these things, especially when He intended prayer to be such a win for His children?

If we are hardwired to pray, then doesn't it make sense that God has provided a way for us to flow with Him in prayer in such a way that we experience His love and see His goodness manifested in real ways? Yes, I believe so!

That's why I want to go on a systematic journey to get a grip on the basics of prayer with you!

B.   LET'S GET A GRIP ON THE BASICS OF PRAYER

Who is this book for? You.

>> If you have never been taught the prayer basics—this book is for *you*.
>> If you have been discouraged by prayers that did not get answered—this book is for *you*.
>> If you are a seasoned pray-er and just need a refresher—this book is for *you*.

Getting a Grip on the Basics of Prayer is a Bible study designed to help you get into your Bible to hear from God and to see what He will speak to you about the subject of prayer! My approach is to help you learn about prayer through a guided, systematic progression of Scriptures, while also being mindful that prayer is not a "system" but a Spirit-led experience with God.

I'm the type of learner who needs to see the big picture *and* the pieces of the puzzle for anything to make sense to me (it doesn't matter if the topic is prayer, golf, or how to cook). At first, seeing all the pieces to the puzzle can be overwhelming, but once I begin to see those things in an organized and practical way, it's much easier to understand and put into practice. In this book, we will look at many prayer puzzle pieces; and at first, it may seem overwhelming, but I am confident that as you go through each chapter, the Lord will help it all come together for you!

In this chapter and the next, I will share several introductory "Prayer Basics" and we will look at answers to "10 Common Questions About Prayer." Then, for the remainder of the book, we will get into numerous Scriptures on specific prayer topics and I encourage you to use the space provided to write down your answers to the questions posed. You will find "Revelation Drops" and testimonies peppered in throughout the book and I will also share my forty-plus years of experience in prayer with the hope that all of this brings clarity to the sometimes "mystical" subject of prayer.

To get the basics on prayer, we will cover the *who, what, when, where, why,* and *how* of prayer in this order:

>> **WHAT:** *What is prayer, and what should we pray about?*

>> **WHO:** *Who should pray and to whom?*

>> **HOW:** *How do we "pray by the rules" to experience answers to prayer?*

>> **WHY:** *Why should we pray, and what happens if we do not pray?*

>>**WHEN:** *When should we pray, and does timing matter?*

>> **WHERE:** *Where should we pray, and from what positional posture?*

We are going to cover a lot of ground in our time together, so at the end of each chapter I encourage you to write down the Bible verses that stood out to you and the truths stirred your heart? Then, take a moment to pray and put those things into practice.

Jesus wasn't kidding when He promised the joy of answered prayer: *"Most assuredly, I say to you, whatever you ask the Father in My name He will give you. Until now you have asked nothing in My name. Ask, and you will receive, that your joy may be full" (John 16:23,24).*

If your prayer life has been stagnant, boring or mundane, you can leave that behind and get excited about the joy of effective prayer! Prayer doesn't have to be a dutiful or disappointing religious exercise, but rather our prayer life can become an exciting *dialogue* with the Lord.

I can't think of anything I enjoy more than helping hungry people (like you!) connect with God as He helps them to "connect the basic Bible dots." Like Peter, I find great joy and encouragement in teaching you the basics over and over and reminding you of the faith essentials: *"Therefore, I will always remind you about these things—even though you already know them and are standing firm in the truth you have been taught. And it is only right that I should keep on reminding you as long as I live" (2 Peter 1:12,13 NLT).*

By the time you finish, I believe you will find a fresh confidence and freedom in prayer! I believe you will have a more intimate relationship with the Lord. You will have a solid working knowledge of what the Bible says about prayer, and you will have a strong faith framework from which to pray. You will be able to pray with humility, compassion, and faith to access heaven's best. And . . .

C. YOU COULD PLAY A PART IN A PRAYER REVIVAL

Did you know that most of the recorded revivals in history began in prayer?
God has always used ordinary men and women to do extraordinary things. In 1857, the Lord put a burden for revival upon the hearts of men and women, so they prayed. The result was a revival that swept the nation.

This revival, known as the Laymen's Prayer Revival, the Third Great Awakening, or the Prayer Revival of 1857, began in September of that same year on Fulton Street in New York City, a few blocks from what we now know as Ground Zero. A small group of businessmen gathered to pray at the North Dutch Reform Church on Fulton Street.

Jeremiah C. Lanphier, a forty-nine-year old lay minister who was discouraged by the lack of fruit in his ministry, became God's catalyst. Not knowing what else to do and in his despair, he decided to pray. He invited others to join him on that first day when he posted this sign: "Prayer Meeting from 12 to 1 o'clock—Stop for 5, 10, 20 minutes, or the whole hour as your time admits."

At first no one showed up, but then a few businessmen trickled in until they had a whopping six people at the first prayer meeting. It quickly grew, and soon dozens, then hundreds, and eventually thousands of people were praying. The prayer revival grew from just six people on that first day to thousands upon thousands around the nation! Here's a quick synopsis of this revival from the C.S. Lewis Institute:

That small meeting was in no way extraordinary. There was no great outpouring of the spirit of God. Lanphier had no way of knowing that it was the beginning of a great national revival which would sweep an estimated 1 million persons into the kingdom of God. . . .

Looking back, historians can see that conditions were ripe for revival. The Revival of 1800 began a golden age of religious interest. But by 1843, a nation intent upon getting and spending had lost interest in religion. The West had opened up. Gold was discovered in California. Railroad building was a craze. The slavery issue was hot. Fortunes ballooned. Faith diminished. . . .

That very week—on Wednesday, October 14—the nation was staggered by the worst financial panic in its history. Banks closed, men were out of work, families went hungry. The crash no doubt had something to do with the astonishing growth of Lanphier's noon meeting (by now called "the Fulton Street prayer meeting"). In a short time, the Fulton Street meeting had taken over the whole building with crowds of more than 3,000. . . .

It was a revival of prayer. There was no hysteria, no unusual disturbances. Just prayer. . . .

In describing this revival, Charles Finney said: "There is such a general confidence in the prevalence of prayer that the people very extensively seemed to prefer meeting for prayer to meeting for preaching. The general impression seemed to be, 'We have had instruction until we are hardened; it is time for us to pray.'"

The revival rolled on into 1859 and 1860. There is no telling how long it might have lasted if the Civil War had not broken out. Some writers say that it carried right through the war.

When the revival was at high tide through the nation, it was judged that 50,000 persons a week were converted. And the number who joined the churches in 1858 amounted to almost 10 percent of the country's total church membership! If the estimate of one million converts is correct (some say the number is closer to 300,000), that accounts for one-thirtieth of the total United States population of that time—and almost all in one year!

What lesson does this revival teach this generation?

Certainly, it demonstrates again how God can use one dedicated life to work out His purposes. Jeremiah Lanphier is an inspiration to all unsung, seemingly unappreciated church workers everywhere. Surprisingly little has been written about him. He was still connected with the Old Dutch Church twenty-five years after the meeting was founded. At that time (1882), someone wrote of him: "Out of that solitary consecration to the service of Christ, who can tell what results have come?"

The Revival of 1857-58 was the last great national revival.[1]

D. ARE YOU CALLED TO THE KINGDOM FOR SUCH A TIME?

The last great national revival was over 150 years ago! Don't you think it's time for a fresh revival of prayer? Perhaps, like Esther of old or like Jeremiah Lanphier and the everyday prayer warriors that joined him in 1857, you too are "called to the kingdom of God for such a time as this."

Charles Finney described this type of prayer perfectly: "A revival may be expected when Christians have a spirit of prayer for a revival. That is, when they pray as if their hearts were set upon it. When Christians have the spirit of prayer for a revival. When they go about groaning out their hearts' desire. When they have real travail of soul."[2]

If you have been discouraged, disappointed, or disillusioned by the condition of the world around you or by the fruit of your own life and ministry; don't despair. Give extra attention to these prayer basics and see what God will do in your life!

Both ancient and modern history are full of stories and anecdotes on the power of prayer. Others much mightier than I in prayer have written incredible books to teach and inspire us. Throughout this book, I have added quotes from such prayer legends like E.M. Bounds, Charles Finney, Charles Spurgeon, Andrew Murray, as well as recognized prayer leaders from our modern day.

The most expert person on prayer is Jesus Himself, and the most important book on prayer is the Bible, so that's where we will camp out. One thing is for sure—God wants to answer your prayers! He is not trying to keep things from you; He desires to get things to you—His goodness, His salvation, His wisdom, His healing, His provision, His joy, and His life.

Your best days are ahead as you give yourself to prayer!

E. PRAY IT OUT

Before we go any further, let's pause to talk about the most important prayer of all—the prayer of salvation. This prayer is the starting point for being saved and experiencing a personal relationship with the Lord Jesus.

If you don't know the Lord or you are not certain where you will spend eternity after you die, you will be happy to know the Bible says, *"If you confess with your mouth the Lord Jesus and believe in your heart that God has raised Him from the dead, you will be saved. For with the heart one believes unto righteousness, and with the mouth confession is made unto salvation. . . . For whoever calls on the name of the Lord shall be saved"* (Romans 10:9,10,13).

If you have never surrendered your life to the Lordship of Jesus and would like to do so, I'd love to pray with you. This is known as the "salvation prayer" and the most important thing about praying this prayer is your heart. You may not yet understand everything Jesus did for you on the cross, but in your heart you know enough to recognize that you are not perfect—you have sinned and fallen short of God's perfection—and you recognize your need for a Savior. Jesus is that Savior.

To experience His saving power, you do just what the Bible says—you call on Him by confessing with your mouth that Jesus is your Lord and believing in your heart that God raised Him from the dead. When you do that, the Bible says you will be saved. This decision is the beginning of having a personal relationship with your Lord and Savior, Jesus Christ. If you'd like to begin a relationship with Jesus and know for sure that you are saved, let's prayer this salvation prayer together:

"Dear God, I want to know You. I want to be saved. I do believe that Jesus is Your son and that You raised Him from the dead. Today, I call on Your name, Jesus. I surrender my life to You, and I confess that Jesus is Lord—my Lord! Thank You for saving me and forgiving all of my sins. From this day forward, I am a Christian. Lord, help me to know You better and to become the person You created me to be. In Jesus' name, amen."

Now that we are all on the same page, let's get a grip on the basics of prayer.

1. "Revival Born in a Prayer Meeting," C.S. Lewis Institute, Fall 2004, https://www.cslewisinstitute.org/webfm_send/577.

2. "Charles Grandison Finney Quotes," Quote Fancy, May 5, 2021, https://quotefancy.com/quote/1529095/Charles-Grandison-Finney-A-revival-may-be-expected-when-Christians-have-a-spirit-of.

CHAPTER 2:

10 COMMON QUESTIONS ABOUT PRAYER

"Is prayer your steering wheel or your spare tire?"
Corrie Ten Boom

There are a lot of questions when it comes to prayer.

>> *How do I know if my prayers are working?*
>> *Is prayer more than slinging an arrow at a bullseye and hoping it hits?*
>> *Do my prayers make a difference?*
>> *Does God hear everyone's prayers?*
>> *Does it matter to whom I pray?*
>> *Isn't God going to do what He wants to do without my prayers?*
>> *Why do some prayers seem to go unheard and unanswered?*
>> *Am I being selfish when I ask for things?*
>> *Does God talk back when I pray?*
>> *Are there certain prayers God can't or won't answer?*
>> *What will happen if I don't pray?*

Thankfully, in His Word, God has given us answers for every question! Let's get started by tackling a few common questions people have when it comes to prayer. We will answer these questions (and more) in greater detail throughout the rest of the book.

A. QUESTION #1: I PRAYED, BUT GOD DID NOT ANSWER MY PRAYER. WHY?

This is an important question! Often, when we feel as though God did not answer our prayer, we get discouraged, cynical, and mad. We often blame God for not answering our prayers the way we wanted Him to do it. But are there reasons some prayers don't seem to get answered? Yes.

If we will keep a humble, honest and a teachable heart, here are a few reasons to consider:

>> **Are you in unbelief?** This is a big consideration. Everything God does He does in response to belief—or faith. The Bible tells us that without faith, it's impossible to please Him. Faith is essential. However, sometimes, we think we are praying "in faith," but really, we are praying "in hope." While hope is great and a first step toward faith—it is not faith. Faith is what God has promised to answer.

What's the difference? When we are "in faith," we *know* we have the petition we have requested.

It's a done deal. When we are "in hope," we *hope* God will answer our prayer soon. *Faith is now. Hope is future.* This is a small yet huge distinction. So, sometimes the best thing to do when we are not in faith, but in hope (and wrestling with doubts and unbelief) is to **NOT** pray—but rather, get into the Word until hope turns to faith—and faith fills our hearts. Then we can pray!

The Bible tells us that if we ask God for something and are double-minded or in doubt, we shouldn't expect to receive anything at all: *"If any of you lacks wisdom, let him ask of God, who gives to all liberally and without reproach, and it will be given to him. But let him ask in faith, with no doubting, for he who doubts is like a wave of the sea driven and tossed by the wind. For let not that man suppose that he will receive anything from the Lord; he is a double-minded man, unstable in all his ways" (James 1:5-8).* Thankfully, we can fix the unbelief problem by doubling up in the Bible and allowing God and His Word to fill our hearts with faith.

>> **Do you lack humility?** This is another biggie. Sometimes our prayers are not from a place of humility, but from a place of entitlement. While the Lord loves to bless us as His children, He resists the proud. It's hard to get answers from God when we are proud and God is resisting us! Here is what James the brother of Jesus says, *"'God resists the proud, but gives grace to the humble.' Therefore submit to God. Resist the devil and he will flee from you. Draw near to God and He will draw near to you" (James 4:6-8).* The good news is that we can fix a pride problem by humbling ourselves before the Lord and others.

>> **Are you walking in love?** When we are not walking in love toward others, our own hearts know it. We feel a sense of condemnation within because we know we are harboring unforgiveness, bitterness, anger, resentment, or ill will toward another person. When we have any of these things in our heart our faith is hindered, the Bible tells us, *"Beloved, if our heart does not condemn us, we have confidence toward God. And whatever we ask we receive from Him, because we keep His commandments and do those things that are pleasing in His sight. And this is His commandment: that we should believe on the name of His Son Jesus Christ and love one another, as He gave us commandment" (1 John 3:21-23).* Thankfully, we can fix this prayer hindrance by forgiving and loving. We don't have to love what others have done, but we can choose to forgive and love them as He has loved us. When we do this, our heart won't condemn us, and we will have confidence in prayer.

>> **Is your request selfish?** When we pray about things with selfish motives, God cannot answer our prayers. For example, we once talked to a woman who wanted to pray God would give her another woman's husband! Everything about that request is selfish, and of course God would not answer it. Most of us would not pray something so obviously selfish, but it's a good practice to check our own hearts when we pray to clean out any selfish motives. Listen to James 4:2-3 NLT, *"You are jealous of what others have, but you can't get it, so you fight and wage war to take it away from them. Yet you don't have what you want because you don't ask God for it. And even when you ask, you don't get it because your motives are all wrong—you want only what will give you pleasure."*

>> **Are you praying according to God's will?** When we pray for something that is not God's will, He won't hear our request, and He cannot answer it. If we pray for something and we don't know if it is God's will, it's hard to have faith (the best we can have is hope) and again, God doesn't answer the prayers of hope; He answers the prayers of faith. Often, we pray too quickly from our emotions, anger, anxieties, or frustrations rather than from faith and knowing God's will. But, if we will take

time to get into God's Word to discover His will for areas of our lives, we can pray prayers that He can answer: *"Now this is the confidence that we have in Him, that if we ask anything according to His will, He hears us. And if we know that He hears us, whatever we ask, we know that we have the petitions that we have asked of Him"* (1 John 5:14,15).

>> **Are you in a lifestyle of sin?** Thank God that because of Jesus our sins are forgiven, and we've been made "the righteousness of God in Christ." Because of Jesus, our sins (past, present, and future) have been forgiven, so we can live in the freedom from condemnation this brings! However, if we want to live in sin (not what we define as sin but what God defines as sin), we have to ask ourselves—why? Why would we want to displease the very One who took the punishment our sin deserved and has extended His grace and mercy to us? Furthermore, if we choose to live in sin (the thing that caused Jesus to go to the cross), should we expect Him to answer our prayers?

David experienced this dichotomy. After living in the sin of adultery and murder, his heart was full of guilt that weighed him down. Finally, he confessed his sin, and God forgave him. His heart was freed from sin and guilt, and after that it was easy for him to experience the joy of answered prayer, *"Oh, what joy for those whose disobedience is forgiven, whose sin is put out of sight!"* (Psalm 32:1 NLT)

The Apostle Paul asks, *"Well then, should we keep on sinning so that God can show us more and more of His wonderful grace? Of course not! Since we have died to sin, how can we continue to live in it?"* (Romans 6:1,2 NLT) If we don't have an inherent desire to forsake sin and live a life that pleases the Lord, we may need to question the validity of our faith and salvation experience. *"We know that God does not hear the prayers of sinners, but if anyone is a worshipper of God and does His will, God hears him"* (John 9:31). God loves us, but He does not wink at sin. Thankfully, Jesus paid the wage our sin deserved, and now we can repent and turn to the Lord at any time—then we can pray with confidence from a pure heart free from condemnation.

>> **Is there disunity in your marriage?** Interestingly, Peter tells us this, *"Husbands, likewise, dwell with them with understanding, giving honor to the wife, as to the weaker vessel, and as being heirs together of the grace of life, that your prayers may not be hindered"* (1 Peter 3:7). When husbands (and wives) don't live with one another in an understanding way—by understanding their differences and giving honor to one another—they do not access the "grace of life" God has provided for their marriage, so their prayers are hindered. If you are married, the best thing to do if you want your prayers to be answered is to understand, honor, and love your spouse.

B.   QUESTION #2: I AM SINGLE; CAN I CLAIM SOMEONE TO BE MY HUSBAND OR WIFE?

The short answer is *yes* and *no*. If you are single and desire to be married, you can definitely pray and ask God for a spouse! But you can't claim a particular person to be your spouse. After all, they have a free will too, what if they don't want to claim you?

When it comes to praying for your spouse, the good news is that you can ask God for the very best spouse for you, and you can pray that you would be the very best spouse for them. You can ask the Lord for a person with the godly traits you desire and then be certain to pray for these same traits in your own life. In other words, you shouldn't pray for God to send you a spouse with a "10 rating" for their success, work ethic and faith if you are acting like someone with a "3 rating" for being lazy, undisciplined, and double-minded. The best thing to do is to be like the spouse you are praying for.

Let me encourage you to pray along the lines of this passage in Isaiah 34. *"Search from the book of the LORD, and read: not one of these shall fail; not one shall lack her mate. For My mouth has commanded it, and His Spirit has gathered them" (Isaiah 34:16).* While this verse describes God's faithfulness to His prophetic Word, the general principle of God's plan for your mate is in there too. So, go ahead and ask God for your mate and trust that by His Spirit He will gather you to your spouse.

Not only can you *pray for a spouse*, you can *pray for your spouse*! Since God knows everything about your future, He knows who your spouse is, even if He has not revealed it to you quite yet. That means you can pray for them before you know them by praying the Scriptures over him or her. I prayed the prayers in Ephesians 1:14-20, Ephesians 3:14-20 and Colossians 1:9-12 over my husband Jeff for years before I ever met him, and God answered exceedingly above my prayers. He will do it for you, too!

C. QUESTION #3: I WANT A BABY; CAN I PRAY FOR GOD TO GIVE US A SON OR DAUGHTER?

You can definitely pray for a baby! There are many dynamics when it comes to praying for a baby, and whether you conceive, adopt, foster, or employ fertility options; here are several scriptures you can pray for yourself and your baby.

>> **Psalm 113:9** *"He grants the barren woman a home, like a joyful mother of children. Praise the LORD!"*

>> **Psalm 127:3-5** *"Behold, children are a heritage from the LORD, the fruit of the womb is a reward. Like arrows in the hand of a warrior, so are the children of one's youth. Happy is the man who has his quiver full of them."*

>> **1 Samuel 1:8-18** *"Then Elkanah her husband said to her, 'Hannah, why do you weep? Why do you not eat? And why is your heart grieved? Am I not better to you than ten sons?' So Hannah arose after they had finished eating and drinking in Shiloh. Now Eli the priest was sitting on the seat by the doorpost of the tabernacle of the LORD. And she was in bitterness of soul, and prayed to the LORD and wept in anguish. Then she made a vow and said, 'O LORD of hosts, if You will indeed look on the affliction of Your maidservant and remember me, and not forget Your maidservant, but will give Your maidservant a male child, then I will give him to the LORD all the days of his life, and no razor shall come upon his head.' And it happened, as she continued praying before the LORD, that Eli watched her mouth. Now Hannah spoke in her heart; only her lips moved, but her voice was not heard. Therefore Eli thought she was drunk. So Eli said to her, 'How long will you be drunk? Put your wine away from you!' But Hannah answered and said, 'No, my lord, I am a woman of sorrowful spirit. I have drunk neither wine nor intoxicating drink, but have poured out my soul before the LORD. Do not consider your maidservant a wicked woman, for out of the abundance of my complaint and grief I have spoken until now.' Then Eli answered and said, 'Go in peace, and the God of Israel grant your petition which you have asked of Him.' And she said, 'Let your maidservant find favor in your sight.' So the woman went her way and ate, and her face was no longer sad."*

When it comes to praying specifically for a boy or a girl, there is not any Bible precedent to pray for your baby's gender. In the Bible, at times, God revealed the baby's gender to someone before they gave birth and in these cases, it was easy for them to pray and expect what God had promised. We see this with Mary and Elizabeth—God told them they were each having a son.

If God were to tell you that you are having a son or a daughter, of course, it's easy pray for that son or daughter. However, over the years, we have known couples who were "claiming" a particular gender for their baby, and when the baby was born as the opposite of what they had prayed for, instead of it being a time of joy and celebration, they had to deal with the grief of what they weren't going to have. This is not God's way. That's why it's not a biblical practice to "claim" a boy or girl. God knows what is best for you and for your future children. So, while you can definitely pray for a baby according to God's Word, it's best to leave the gender in His hands.

D. QUESTION #4: I PRAYED FOR SOMEONE ELSE, BUT NOTHING HAPPENED. WHY?

Sometimes we pray for others, yet we don't see results. Why? For example, perhaps you prayed for your grandma or a neighbor to be healed, and then they died—why? Or, maybe you prayed for your brother to get a certain job, but he didn't get it—why? Or, perhaps you prayed for your uncle to stop being mean to your aunt, yet he didn't stop—why? Maybe you've gone to your local hospital or homeless shelter to pray for everyone to be healthy and wealthy, but it didn't work—why?

There are many layers in these types of situations, and none of them are the same. Short of God's sovereign act of mercy in someone's life, there are general prayer principles we can learn when praying for others.

First, as a general rule, as individuals, spouses and parents, we have a degree of authority to pray for our own life and loved ones. However, in the same way that we can't pray and receive someone else's salvation—they must pray their own salvation prayer—so, too, we can't pray and receive God's promises for others. After all, we don't have authority over other people. They have the authority (and responsibility) for their own lives, and we can't use prayer to insert our will or desire to usurp or override theirs.

While we aren't authorized to pray the salvation prayer for someone else, we can pray they hear the gospel through a laborer being sent to them so they can pray the salvation prayer for themselves. We aren't authorized to pray for an entire hospital to be healed and emptied out, but we can pray for the those who are sick to hear the good news of Jesus (just like the woman with the issue of blood in Mark 5) so they can believe His words and receive Him and His wisdom and healing power. Can you see that?

Second, when it comes to praying for others, it's often best to prayer the "prayer of agreement." In doing so, we can ask them what they desire, and then we can pray and agree together in faith for the things we are requesting from God.

Third, when we pray for others there are often other spiritual principles at work. The late Kenneth E. Hagin, a man well known for his life of prayer and faith, has a personal story that drives home this point:

> *"There was a Rhema student years ago who was dying of a tumor. He was under forty years old. Kenneth Hagin [and other ministers] all prayed for him, but he ended up in a coma. Kenneth Hagin immediately went to the Lord in prayer and asked what happened. God's response surprised him.*

19

He told Kenneth, 'Spiritual laws have already been set in motion and cannot be reversed at this time.'

"The man ended up dying, and Kenneth Hagin didn't know what the Lord meant until he attended his funeral. At the service, this man's brother told him that this man had said continually since he was a little boy, 'I'll never live to see forty.' He said it all his life. In fact, the last time he saw his brother, he had said that very thing.

"What was he doing by continually confessing he wouldn't live to see forty? He was setting spiritual laws in motion. Now, he could have turned the situation around, but he came to the point of being in a coma. He set the spiritual laws in motion with his mouth, so he had to turn them around—others couldn't do it for him.

"You protect your circle with your words because words set spiritual laws in motion. If you've spoken wrong words all your life, you can begin reversing them today by repenting and speaking right words. You can say, 'I'll never have heart troubles. I'll never have a disease. I'm going to live a long life. . . . '" [1]

Can you see that sometimes in our eagerness to pray for others, without all the facts, we pray for things outside our scope of authority. It is helpful to know these things; otherwise, we may get discouraged praying for people and seeing a lack of results, especially when we pray for those for whom we do not have any spiritual authority. All of this being said, there are a lot of ways we have been authorized to pray for others. We will cover more in the chapters that follow.

E.   QUESTION #5: WHAT ROLE DOES PATIENCE PLAY WHEN I PRAY?

Patience plays a big role in our prayers. Notice the Bible tells us that through "faith and patience" we inherit the promises of God (Hebrews 6:12). James 1:4 encourages us with this, *"But let patience have its perfect work, that you may be perfect and complete, lacking nothing."* When it comes to prayer, faith and patience are in our control, but timing is in God's control.

F.   QUESTION #6: WHEN I PRAY, DO MY WORDS MAKE ANY DIFFERENCE?

Absolutely! It's impossible to pray in faith in one breath and then speak words of doubt in the next and then expect God to answer your prayers.

For example, we can't go north and south at the same time. We can't go "north" by praying and believing God is answering our request, while at the same time going "south" by saying words that are the opposite of what we prayed. Our words in prayer and our words after we pray need to be congruent words of faith. Notice what James says, *"Out of the same mouth proceed blessing and cursing. My brethren, these things ought not to be so. Does a spring send forth fresh water and bitter from the same opening?"* (James 3:10-11).

What we say (the words we speak or confess) is very, very important. Hebrews 10:23 says, *"Let us hold fast the confession of our hope without wavering, for He who promised is faithful."* The biblical definition of confession means to say what God says, to confess or profess what God says about any given thing. Our words and confession of faith play a really important role when it comes to prayer.

G. QUESTION #7: HOW SHOULD I APPROACH SPIRITUAL WARFARE WHEN I PRAY?

This is a great question. In our study together, you will learn how to pray from an offensive place of victory being seated with Christ in heavenly places.

In the Old Testament book of Daniel, we see a twenty-one day spiritual battle taking place when an angel gave him this message, *"Then he said to me, "Do not fear, Daniel, for from the first day that you set your heart to understand, and to humble yourself before your God, your words were heard; and I have come because of your words. But the prince of the kingdom of Persia withstood me twenty-one days; and behold, Michael, one of the chief princes, came to help me, for I had been left alone there with the kings of Persia. Now I have come to make you understand what will happen to your people in the latter days, for the vision refers to many days yet to come"* (Daniel 10:12-14).

We see how Daniel won the spiritual battle then, but what about now, in the New Testament under the New Covenant?

Now under our New Covenant, Jesus has defeated and disarmed the devil and we are to enforce Satan's defeat in Jesus' name. *"Having disarmed principalities and powers, He made a public spectacle of them, triumphing over them in it"* (Colossians 2:15).

As Christians, we are not to pray scared or defeated prayers, rather we are to exercise our faith to enforce Satan's defeat by praying with the authority Jesus has given us: *"Finally, my brethren, be strong in the Lord and in the power of His might. Put on the whole armor of God, that you may be able to stand against the wiles of the devil. For we do not wrestle against flesh and blood, but against principalities, against powers, against the rulers of the darkness of this age, against spiritual hosts of wickedness in the heavenly places. Therefore take up the whole armor of God, that you may be able to withstand in the evil day, and having done all, to stand. . . . Praying always with all prayer and supplication in the Spirit, being watchful to this end with all perseverance and supplication for all the saints—and for me, that utterance may be given to me, that I may open my mouth boldly to make known the mystery of the gospel, for which I am an ambassador in chains; that in it I may speak boldly, as I ought to speak"* (Ephesians 6:10-13, 18-20). In prayer, we have been given divine weapons for pulling down every stronghold: *"For though we walk in the flesh, we do not war according to the flesh. For the weapons of our warfare are not carnal but mighty in God for pulling down strongholds, casting down arguments and every high thing that exalts itself against the knowledge of God, bringing every thought into captivity to the obedience of Christ."* (2 Corinthians 10:3-5).

H. QUESTION #8: HOW DO I PRAY WHEN I AM CONFUSED ABOUT UNANSWERED PRAYERS?

When you are frustrated, hurt, mad, or confused about prayers that have not gotten answered the way you wanted, it's easy to pull away from the Lord, other believers, and church. The best thing to do is to stay on God's side. He's for you. He's not against you. Lean into the truth that God loves you.

Trust that God sees the bigger picture, and He will reveal anything to you that you need to know. The Bible says, *"The secret things belong to the LORD our God, but those things which are revealed belong to us and to our children forever, that we may do all the words of this law"* (Deuteronomy 29:29).

Remind yourself that the Lord always has your best interests in mind. He will keep secret the things that are His, and He will reveal to you the things He wants you to know.

I. QUESTION #9: WILL GOD ANSWER MY PRAYERS IF I FAST?

The short answer is *no*. The other short answer is that fasting *will help* your flesh to be quieted, your spirit to be strengthened, and your heart to be in a better posture to pray in faith.

When it comes to fasting and prayer, people wonder . . .

>> Does fasting and prayer change us or God?
>> If we fast longer, will God answer our prayers quicker?
>> Is fasting under the Old Covenant the same as fasting under the New Covenant?
>> What is the role of fasting and prayer for New Testament believers?

Fasting does not twist God's arm, and He is not obligated to answer our prayers because we fasted. However, there is a role for fasting, and it has to do with helping our spiritual sensitivity and faith, not with God's willingness to answer. Let's look at this important topic by reading a story in Mark 9:17-29:

"Then one of the crowd answered and said, 'Teacher, I brought You my son, who has a mute spirit. And wherever it seizes him, it throws him down; he foams at the mouth, gnashes his teeth, and becomes rigid. So I spoke to Your disciples, that they should cast it out, but they could not.' He answered him and said, 'O faithless generation, how long shall I be with you? How long shall I bear with you? Bring him to Me.' Then they brought him to Him. And when he saw Him, immediately the spirit convulsed him, and he fell on the ground and wallowed, foaming at the mouth. So He asked his father, 'How long has this been happening to him?' And he said, 'From childhood. And often he has thrown him both into the fire and into the water to destroy him. But if You can do anything, have compassion on us and help us.' Jesus said to him, 'If you can believe, all things are possible to him who believes.' Immediately the father of the child cried out and said with tears, 'Lord, I believe; help my unbelief!' When Jesus saw that the people came running together, He rebuked the unclean spirit, saying to it, 'Deaf and dumb spirit, I command you, come out of him and enter him no more!' Then the spirit cried out, convulsed him greatly, and came out of him. And he became as one dead, so that many said, 'He is dead.' But Jesus took him by the hand and lifted him up, and he arose. And when He had come into the house, His disciples asked Him privately, 'Why could we not cast it out?' So He said to them, 'This kind can come out by nothing but prayer and fasting.'"

Tradition tells us that this is a story about how a mute demon is causing a young boy to have seizures, and that this demon will not leave the boy without prayer and fasting. Is that what Jesus is talking about? Is that conclusion congruent with the rest of Scripture? Let's look.

Notice Jesus says, *"This kind can come out by nothing but prayer and fasting."* What *kind* of what is He talking about? Is this a reference to the mute demon or to something else?

Let's take note of Jesus' words in verse 19—*"faithless generation"*—and His words in verse 23—*"all things are possible to those who believe"*—and the words of the boy's father in verse 24—*"help my unbelief."* All of these phrases tell us this is clearly a story about *faith* and *belief*. This is a story of how to overcome the kind of unbelief that is being manifest! This is not a story about demons or deliverance; the actual story is one of faith and unbelief.

When we fast and pray, we are not twisting God's arm or somehow doing sacrificial penance to persuade Him to deliver us, nor are we trying to convince the devil to leave us alone. Rather, when we fast and pray, we are quieting our flesh and allowing our spirit to become more sensitive to the things of God. As our spirit is more dominant, unbelief goes. It is faith in the name of Jesus that casts out demons, not prayer and fasting; but prayer and fasting causes this *kind* of unbelief to leave so faith can operate! Can you see that?

I like the way Pastor Creflo A. Dollar puts it: *"Prayer and fasting doesn't move the devil or God! It has nothing to do with convincing God or the devil of anything and EVERYTHING to do with building our faith, trust, and reliance on God. Prayer and fasting is about dealing with our own unbelief!"* [2]

Kenneth E. Hagin encourages living a "fasted life." The idea is that rather than doing periodic fasts of three, seven, or twenty-one days; or fasting pleasant foods; instead we adopt a daily discipline of fasting to keep our flesh under and our spirit sensitive to God by controlling our appetites. That means developing the habit of not overindulging in foods (or any other substance) that would want to dominate us. That way we stay spiritually sharp and full of faith.

So, what's the bottom line? *Don't fast and pray* to convince God to do something for you, but rather *do fast and pray* to quiet your flesh, increase your spiritual sensitivity, and build your faith in God's Word.

J. QUESTION #10: WHEN I LOOK AT THE WORLD AROUND ME, HOW SHOULD I PRAY?

Often when we look at the world around us—governments, education, business, big tech, family, spirituality, sexuality, morality and more—we can feel very small and unsure about how to pray. Thankfully, God gave us this encouragement in Romans 8:26-28 NLT, *"And the Holy Spirit helps us in our weakness. For example, we don't know what God wants us to pray for. But the Holy Spirit prays for us with groanings that cannot be expressed in words. And the Father who knows all hearts knows what the Spirit is saying, for the Spirit pleads for us believers in harmony with God's own will. And we know that God causes everything to work together for the good of those who love God and are called according to His purpose for them."*

When we don't know how to pray, the Holy Spirit will help us! He helps us to pray "with our understanding" and "with our spirit," to pray according to God's perfect will. The best thing to do when you feel overwhelmed and helpless is to pray in the Spirit, knowing He is helping you to pray out His will. (In this study, we will talk more about how to pray even when you don't know how to pray.)

Not only does the Lord help us to pray when we don't know how—but He expects us to do so. As believers, we have a responsibility to use the authority Jesus has given us, to pray for those in our sphere of influence, and to declare His will to be done on earth as it is in heaven. When we don't know how to pray for the world around us, we should not shrink back, but we should lean on the Holy Spirit to pray bold prayers in Jesus' name! We can be encouraged in knowing that believers around the world are praying for their spheres of influence and the world at large—together in prayer, we can make a difference!

K.   PRAY IT OUT

I hope some of your questions were answered and I hope you are being stirred up to pray! Before we head into the next chapter, let me pray for you. This prayer found in Colossians 1:9-12 NLT:

> *"I have not stopped praying for you since I first heard about you, dear reader. I ask God to give you complete knowledge of his will and to give you spiritual wisdom and understanding. Then the way you live will always honor and please the Lord, and your life will produce every kind of good fruit. All the while, you will grow as you learn to know God better and better. I also pray that you will be strengthened with all his glorious power so you will have all the endurance and patience you need. May you be filled with joy, and always thanking the Father. In Jesus' name. amen."*

Let's go!

1. "The Circle of Blessing.," Kenneth Copeland Ministries Blog, December 5, 2019, https://blog.kcm.org/the-circle-of-blessing/.

2. Creflo Dollar Ministries, "Prayer and fasting doesn't move the Devil or God! It has nothing to do with convincing God or the Devil of anything and EVERY-THING to do with building our faith, trust and reliance on God. #creflodollar #faithandtrust #prayerandbelief," Facebook, April 19, 2021, https://www.facebook.com/CrefloDollarMinistries/posts/325212928954567.

SECTION 2:

THE "WHAT" OF PRAYER

CHAPTER 3:

THE "WHAT" OF PRAYER - PART 1

"Prayer is the slender nerve that moves the muscles of omnipotence."
Charles Spurgeon

To get a grip on the basics of prayer, let's start by answering this basic question: "What is prayer?"

Prayer puts legs to our Christian life. Without prayer, the Christian life is an accumulation of knowledge, rituals, and theory; but with prayer, the Christian life becomes a fulfilling, two-way communication with the living God!

Jesus' brother, James, may have given us the best definition of prayer, *"The effective, fervent prayer of a righteous man avails much" (James 5:16).* The Classic Amplified Bible puts it this way, *"The earnest (heartfelt, continued) prayer of a righteous man makes tremendous power available [dynamic in its working]."* Prayer, when done right, is effective, heartfelt communication with God that makes tremendous power available!

Can you see that prayer is a powerful, multi-dimensional, loving dialogue with God? What else do we know about prayer?

>> Prayer is a divine exchange with the Lord.
>> Prayer is the language of the heart—our human heart to the heart of God.
>> Prayer is the way we communicate with heaven to accomplish God's plans on earth.
>> Prayer is the loving expression of friendship between trusted friends—God and man.
>> Prayer is a vehicle for requesting the things we need from the God who desires to give them to us.

Campus Crusade for Christ founder, the late Dr. Bill Bright, captured a wonderful overarching definition of prayer when he described it this way, *"Prayer is simply communicating with God. . . . It is a dialogue between two people who love each other—God and man."*[1]

What does that kind of prayer look like? Let's find out.

A. PRAYER IS NOT A COOKIE-CUTTER EXERCISE

Just as we communicate from our hearts with one another in a variety of ways—talking, whispering, shouting, crying, and more—so, too, we can communicate with the Lord. In order to have an effective prayer life, it's good to know that we don't have to conform to a "cookie-cutter" style of praying. When we talk to our heavenly Father from a place of respect and within the boundaries of His Word, we will enjoy intimacy with Him, answers to our requests, and the satisfaction of fruit that remains.

Before we get into what prayer is, let's talk about what prayer *isn't.*

>> Prayer isn't anxious begging; although, it is heartfelt.

>> Prayer isn't whining; although, faith-filled tears may be involved.

>> Prayer isn't just good thoughts; although, our thoughts are important.

>> Prayer isn't a formula; although, God has given us His instructions.

>> Prayer isn't flowery speech; although, we are addressing the King of kings.

>> Prayer isn't preaching, although, our prayers can be passionate.

>> Prayer isn't good vibes; although, prayer makes us feel good.

>> Prayer isn't a mental exercise, although we do engage our minds.

>> Prayer isn't a feeling; although, our emotions play a role.

>> Prayer isn't superstitious; although, we pray to bring invisible things into the visible realm.

>> Prayer isn't a rabbit's foot or lucky charm; although, we certainly feel blessed when prayers are answered.

If these things describe what prayer *isn't*; then, what *is* prayer?

When we boil it all down, prayer can be divided into these three categories:

1. **Prayer gives us a way to enjoy fellowship with God.**
2. **Prayer gives us a way to request things from God.**
3. **Prayer gives us a way to produce lasting fruit for God.**

Are you ready to get into the details and dig deeper into each of these three categories? Here's where we start the workbook part of our Bible study. This is your chance to read the Scriptures and prayerfully answer each question in the space provided. As a reminder, unless otherwise noted all of the scriptures listed in the workbook sections of each chapter are from the New King James Version of the Bible. If you need more room to write down your answers to the questions, you may want to use a separate notebook or journal.

B. PRAYER GIVES US A WAY TO ENJOY FELLOWSHIP WITH GOD

Through prayer, we can have a personal and intimate relationship with the Lord.

1. **Psalm 5:2**
   "Give heed to the voice of my cry, my King and my God, for to You I will pray."

   Who hears the cry of your voice?

   To whom do you pray?

2. **Psalm 27:4**
   "One thing I have desired of the LORD, that will I seek: that I may dwell in the house of the LORD all the days of my life, to behold the beauty of the LORD, and to inquire in His temple."

   What one thing should you seek?

How would you describe the "beauty of the Lord"?

REVELATION DROP: Prayer gives us the opportunity to enjoy fellowship with God—and to behold the beauty of the Lord. The phrase "the beauty of the Lord" has been rolling around in my spirit for some time, yet for many years I didn't know what it meant. As the Holy Spirit revealed more of Jesus—His love, His joy and His goodness—to me, I began to see that Jesus IS the beauty of the Lord. He is the visible image of the invisible God—the God whose loving-kindness is better than life. Prayer allows us to know Him and His beauty more intimately.

>> The "beauty of the Lord" is found in the selfless life of Jesus and the redemptive plan of God.

>> The "beauty of the Lord" was seen through Jesus' compassion and healing power at the gate called Beautiful (Acts 3) when a crippled man was healed in His Name.

>> The "beauty of the Lord" is seen through us, His followers. When we share the Gospel, we become those with "beautiful feet" who bring good news (Romans 10:15).

>> I see the "beauty of the Lord" in His creation—colors, patterns, design, shapes, smells, tastes, and texture—all of these have become more meaningful to me. When I think about the attention to beautiful details God put into His creation just to bless us, He becomes even more beautiful to me.

>> But here's the part that was a surprise to me—through a dream the Lord gave me one night, I saw "the beauty of the Lord" in His utter delight while He watches us, His children, enjoying His artistic creation! Yes, Jesus is delighted in our delight. When we enjoy and appreciate Him and His creation, He is happy to see us happy.

In prayer, as we fellowship with God the Father, Jesus the Son and the Holy Spirit, we get to see the beauty of the Lord!

3.   **Psalm 73:25 TPT**
"Whom have I in heaven but You? You're all I want! No one on earth means as much to me as you."

How does this passage speak to your heart?

4.   **Psalm 42:1**
"As the deer pants for the water brooks, so pants my soul for You, O God. My soul thirsts for God, for the living God."

Circle the key words *pants* and *thirsts*.

Describe a time when you panted or thirsted for God:

How can you increase your thirst for God?

5. **Psalm 63:1-6 NLT**
"O God, you are my God; I earnestly search for you. My soul thirsts for you; my whole body longs for you in this parched and weary land where there is no water. I have seen you in your sanctuary and gazed upon your power and glory. Your unfailing love is better than life itself; how I praise you! I will praise you as long as I live, lifting up my hands to you in prayer."

In what way does the psalmist search for God?

What causes the psalmist to want to praise and pray?

REVELATION DROP: It is said of Susanna Wesley. a woman who sought God and the mother of famous hymn writers, Charles and John Wesley, that she seldom gave the Lord less than a full hour a day in prayer. She was the mother of nineteen children, so when it was time for her personal prayer with the Lord, she would take her apron and pull it up over her head for her prayer time. Her children were instructed to never interrupt mother while she was praying. She knew she needed that personal prayer base for life.

6. **Hebrews 10:22**
"Let us draw near with a true heart in full assurance of faith, having our hearts sprinkled from an evil conscience and our bodies washed with pure water."

In what way should you draw near to God?

When it comes to faith, what type of faith should you have?

When it comes to your heart, how does God see your heart?

REVELATION DROP: We can draw near to God with faith and boldness because of the finished work of Jesus on the cross. Our ability to approach the Lord in prayer with full assurance is not based on our righteousness, but it is based on His—the free gift of righteousness He has given to us! The enemy likes to use condemnation, shame, and a sense of unworthiness to keep us from praying; but as believers, we have been washed and given free access to draw near to God's throne of grace (Hebrews 4:16). At His throne, we can pray and fellowship with the Lord, request all that we need from Him, and work with the Lord in prayer to further His purposes. What a privilege!

C. PRAYER GIVES US A WAY TO MAKE REQUESTS OF GOD

Prayer gives us a way to make requests of God. We see this in Jesus' life and teachings to the disciples.

In fact, have you ever thought about the fact that Jesus never told His disciples that it was not His will to answer prayer? In fact, quite the opposite! Over and over, Jesus reiterated the Father's heart to answer prayer and to give good things to those who pray.

1.   **Matthew 7:7-11**

"Ask, and it will be given to you; seek, and you will find; knock, and it will be opened to you. For everyone who asks receives, and he who seeks finds, and to him who knocks it will be opened. Or what man is there among you who, if his son asks for bread, will give him a stone? Or if he asks for a fish, will he give him a serpent? If you then, being evil, know how to give good gifts to your children, how much more will your Father who is in heaven give good things to those who ask Him!"

What does God promise to those who ask?

According to these verses, how much does God want to bless those who ask?

2.   **John 16:23-24**

"And in that day you will ask Me nothing. Most assuredly, I say to you, whatever you ask the Father in My name He will give you. Until now you have asked nothing in My name. Ask, and you will receive, that your joy may be full."

To whom should you *not direct* your prayers?

To whom do you *direct* your prayers?

In whose name do you pray?

What is your role in prayer?

What will the Father do?

What is the result of receiving answered prayers?

REVELATION DROP: There are several huge revelations in this passage. Jesus gives us the definition and all of the ingredients for New Testament prayer in this verse.

First, Jesus wants us to pray to the Father. Jesus tells us *we will* direct our prayers to the Father in Jesus' name. Jesus also tells us *we will not* direct our prayers to Him. Effective prayer is prayed to the Father *in* Jesus' name. When it comes to this prayer of making requests, Jesus tells us to pray *to* the Father in His Name by the power of the Holy Spirit.

Second, Jesus wants us to ask. Let's look at another key word—*ask*. What is the meaning of the word *ask*?

The original New Testament is written in Greek, and the Greek word for *ask* is translated into English in the Bible in a variety of ways. One time in the Bible, *ask* is translated as "call for," and two times it's translated as "require."[2] I like both of those in this context. When we pray to the Father in Jesus' name, we can "call for" and "require" what He has promised.

Third, Jesus wants our joy to be full! He said we could ask for whatever we need, and He would give it to us so that our joy would be made full!

3. **Matthew 21:22**
    "And whatever things you ask in prayer, believing, you will receive."

    What can you ask for in prayer?

    What heart posture needs to accompany your prayers?

    If you ask in prayer with a believing heart, what will happen?

4. **John 15:7**
    "If you abide in Me, and My words abide in you, you will ask what you desire, and it shall be done for you."

    What does Jesus say you can pray for?

    What does Jesus say the prerequisites are?

    What does Jesus promise will be done?

    Can you see how generous God wants to be toward you?

D. PRAYER GIVES US A WAY TO PRODUCE FRUIT FOR GOD

What a privilege to work together with God in prayer, to produce fruit that will remain.

1. **John 15:16**
    "I chose you, and appointed you, that you should go and bear fruit, and that your fruit should

remain, that whatever you ask of the Father in My name, He may give to you."

What did Jesus choose and appoint you to do?

What does Jesus say you could ask for?

What does Jesus promise will happen?

2. **Ephesians 3:20-21 AMPC**

"Now to Him Who, by (in consequence of) the [action of His] power that is at work within us, is able to [carry out His purpose and] do superabundantly, far over and above all that we [dare] ask or think [infinitely beyond our highest prayers, desires, thoughts, hopes, or dreams]—To Him be glory in the church and in Christ Jesus throughout all generations forever and ever. Amen (so be it)."

What is God able to do for those who dare to ask?

To what degree does God want to answer your "highest prayers"?

Who gets all the glory forever and ever?

REVELATION DROP: I remember reading this passage as a young Christian. I was so inspired to pray big prayers! I knew Jesus wanted us to make disciples, and I wanted to tell everyone about Him, so I prayed this prayer: *"Father, I pray that You help me to help people know You. I want to fulfill my God-given potential to produce fruit that remains for your glory and honor. I ask You, Lord, to help me reach people, make disciples and influence a minimum of one million people for You. In Jesus' name, amen."*

At the time, I was a sophomore in college majoring in biology with hopes of becoming a dentist and I think the sphere of my influence for the Lord was limited to my three sisters, my mom and stepdad, and my dad and stepmom—a total of seven people! Nevertheless, the Lord told us to pray and believe He would do exceedingly above our highest prayers. I figured making disciples and reaching one million people for Christ would be a goal way beyond my wildest dreams.

Little did I know that over the next forty years, the Lord would call me into the ministry (not to dentistry!) and lead me to write discipleship books, produce a television program, and co-pastor a church with my husband where we would have the chance to influence people for Christ. I don't know if I've hit the million-person mark yet, but I have no doubt the course my life has taken is directly connected to that big prayer.

What big prayers are you praying? The best part of praying big prayers is that Jesus gets the glory and you get the benefit—the benefit of working with God on eternal things.

Are you being inspired to see prayer in these three ways?

>> Prayer gives you as a way to enjoy fellowship with God.
>> Prayer gives you a way to request things from God.
>> Prayer gives you a way to produce lasting fruit for God.

I love what E.M. Bounds, legendary author on prayer, said, *"There is no proof so clear and demonstrative that God exists than prayer and its answers."*[3] The revivalist Charles Finney described the importance of prayer best when he said, *"Unless I had the spirit of prayer, I could do nothing."*[4]

E. PRAY IT OUT

What verse or passages stood out to you in this chapter? What truths stirred your heart?

Take a moment to pray and put these things into practice.

1. Bill Bright, How to Pray (Orlando: Campus Crusade for Christ, Inc., 1971), 7.

2. Blue Letter Bible, s.v. "G154 - aiteō," accessed March 10, 2021, https://www.blueletterbible.org//lang/lexicon/lexicon.cfm?Strongs=G154&t=KJV.

3. E. M. Bounds, The Possibilities of Prayer (Grand Rapids: Baker Book House, 1979), 86.

4. "16 Charles Finney Quotes," Christian Quotes, May 5, 2021, https://www.christianquotes.info/quotes-by-author/charles-finney-quotes/.

CHAPTER 4:

THE "WHAT" OF PRAYER - PART 2

*"As is the business of tailors to make clothes and cobblers to make shoes,
so it is the business of Christians to pray."*
Martin Luther

In the same way that our communication with one another is diverse, so, too, our prayer communication with the Lord can be expressed in many ways. When we need encouragement, we pray. In times of crisis, we pray. When we are tempted to be fearful, we pray. During a national tragedy, there are designated days of prayer. As believers, we pray for our presidents and prime ministers. We pray for our friends and families, our kids, our spouses, our soldiers, our doctors, our pastors, and even our enemies. We pray for those who are hurting. We pray for those who help the hurting. We pray over our biggest decisions. We pray over the smallest details. What a privilege it is to pray.

When it comes to our study of the "what" of prayer, there are still many legitimate questions.

>> Is prayer a matter of twisting the Lord's arm to do what we want Him to do?
>> Is prayer pleading with Him to do something He doesn't want to do?
>> Is prayer more than talking with God to ask, appropriate, make a request, or place an order?
>> Is prayer a personal and private discipline, or a public and purpose-filled obligation?
>> Is prayer a monologue or a two-way communication with the living God?
>> Is prayer supposed to be silent, loud, an internal conversation or an audible one?

Understanding the "what" of prayer will set us up for a powerful and fruitful life. Let's look at several more pieces of the "prayer puzzle."

A. PRAYER IS EXPRESSED IN MANY WAYS

Talking to God can take on many forms. Sometimes, we pray for the sheer joy of fellowshipping with the Lord; we aren't asking for anything. At other times, we pray to ask and make specific requests for ourselves or others. Still other times, we pray as if we are in a strategy room flowing with the Holy Spirit to produce fruit and bring God's will to pass on earth as it is in heaven. To get an overview of the scope and types of prayer, let's look at several passages.

1. **Prayer is a round-the-clock experience—Psalm 55:17.**
   "Evening and morning and at noon I will pray, and cry aloud, and He shall hear my voice."

   When can you pray?

What does God hear?

2. **Prayer is a secret-place privilege—Matthew 6:6.**
"But you, when you pray, go into your room, and when you have shut your door, pray to your Father who is in the secret place; and your Father who sees in secret will reward you openly."

What does "secret place" mean to you?

What has God promised to do "openly"?

Do you have a secret place where you like to pray? Where? (It can be your closet, your bathtub, your car, under your blankets, on a walk or sitting in a park and quietly talking to God within your own heart.)

3. **Prayer is the midnight-hour remedy—Acts 16:25.**
"But at midnight Paul and Silas were praying and singing hymns to God, and the prisoners were listening to them."

What do Paul and Silas do at the midnight hour?

Is their prayer loud or silent? (How do you know?)

REVELATION DROP: When you face your hardest moments, midnight-hour prayer is vital. Praying and singing are both forms of prayer. Singing is communicating with God in praise and melody. Billy Graham expressed this well, *"I believe that the greatest form of prayer is praise to God."* [1]

If you are facing a "midnight hour" of difficulty or challenge, there is nothing better than focusing your heart on the Lord as you begin to pray and sing. Some of the most meaningful prayer times I have had with the Lord have been when I faced deep disappointment or discouragement as I pursued His plan for my life. In those moments, praying and singing go hand in hand.

I will never forget a season of pioneering our church and being eight months pregnant with our fourth child while living in a small and dingy little rental cottage. I was so discouraged! I wondered if we had missed God entirely as we planted a church. During that time, I made a decision to pray and sing to the Lord. I remember walking around our home many times singing a Scripture-memory song from Psalm 86:12, then recorded by Integrity Music. The melody and these simple words lifted me in that season: *"I will praise you, Lord my God, with all my heart; I will glorify your name forever."*

As I poured out my heart to the Lord, my prayers, singing, and tears flowed freely, and I knew

He heard me and loved me. Over the months that followed, He poured hope, encouragement and divine answers back into my life. But the best part is the memory I have of that sweet time with the Lord. I hope you will throw caution to the wind and pour out your heart to the Lord in prayer and singing.

4. **Prayer is presenting your case—Isaiah 43:25-26 NLT.**
   "I—yes, I alone—will blot out your sins for my own sake and will never think of them again. Let us review the situation together, and you can present your case to prove your innocence."

   What does this passage tell you about reviewing the situation together and presenting your case to the Lord?

   Do you have a "situation" you'd like to review with the Lord?

   REVELATION DROP: When it comes to prayer, we can pray like an attorney and present our case. Someone once said, *"Argumentative prayers are the best kind of praying."* God seems to like it when we argue our case by presenting His Word to Him and praying passionately and intelligently.

5. **Prayer is a good morning habit—Mark 1:35.**
   "Now in the morning, having risen a long while before daylight, He went out and departed to a solitary place; and there He prayed."

   What three things do you learn about prayer in this passage?

   Jesus prayed at this time:

   Jesus went to this place:

   Jesus did this:

   What does your daily habit of prayer look like (or what should it look like)?

   What time could you get up to spend with the Lord?

6. **Prayer is the way to bear fruit that remains—John 15:16 NASB.**
   "You did not choose Me, but I chose you and appointed you that you would go and bear fruit, and that your fruit would remain, so that whatever you ask the Father in My name He may give you."

   Who do you ask in prayer?

   In whose name do you pray?

What has God promised?

REVELATION DROP: I have always loved this passage because it seems like such a privilege to be chosen and appointed by Jesus to go, pray, and bear fruit. Not only did Jesus choose and appoint us to be fruitful; He gave us the gift of prayer to bring forth that fruit! We can pray in a way that eternal, lasting fruit is produced. Your prayers make an eternal difference!

I remember a profound prayer experience I had along these lines. I had just completed writing my first book, *Getting a Grip on the Basics*, and I didn't know what to do next. As I was making a five-hour car trip to go speak at a church, I began to pray and asked the Lord to use the book to further His purposes.

I prayed, "Lord, I ask You to use this book and get it into the hands of anyone in America who needs to be established in the basics of their faith. Lord, use it to help Your church and to build up Your body. In Jesus' name, amen."

I sensed the Lord speaking to my heart, "Why stop with America?"

"Okay, Lord, I ask You to use this book and get it into the hands of anyone who speaks English and who needs to be established in the basics of their faith. Lord use it to help Your church and to build up Your body. In Jesus' name, amen."

Again, I felt the Lord speaking to my heart, "Why stop with English?"

I smiled. "Okay, Father, I ask You to use this book and get it into the hands of anyone, anywhere on planet Earth and in any language You see fit, to strengthen them in the basics of their faith. Lord, use it to help Your church and to build up Your body. In Jesus' name, amen."

That was the end of my prayer time and I continued on my journey that day.

Now, over thirty years later, the Lord's answer to that prayer is evident. He has seen fit to get this book into multiple nations around the world by prompting people to translate it into over twenty-five languages and counting. The funny thing is that this book has never been a New York Times Best Seller, and most people wouldn't even know this book exists, but with more than 250,000 English copies circulating, it's been producing eternal fruit; and it is still going to nations, villages, and homes I'll never visit this side of heaven.

I have often wondered what would have happened had I not prayed and simply asked according to Jesus' words? What about you? What prayer should you pray?

7. **Prayer is an all-night experience—Luke 6:12.**
    "Now it came to pass in those days that He went out to the mountain to pray, and continued all night in prayer to God."

When, where, and how long did Jesus pray?

REVELATION DROP: Prayer can be an all-night experience! After this night in prayer, Jesus selected His twelve disciples, and their selection would impact the eternal history of mankind and the church. Maybe Jesus prayed all night to get clarity on who to select. Or perhaps, Jesus prayed all night for the sheer joy of fellowship with His Father. Either way, as He leads you, there are times to pray all night!

Stephen Nielsen describes this passage in his wonderful book *Basics of Prayer*: *"Most of us would regard this kind of prayer (Luke 6:12) as particularly earnest and sacrificial—I mean, it would be something that was hard to do. But if we look at it in the light that Jesus loved His Father and longed to be with Him, we get an entirely different idea. This all-night-prayer of Jesus' I think was joyous and refreshing. That is because His prayer was made up of a strong desire that put all other desires in second place, even the desire for sleep."* [2]

8. **Prayer is a thankful lifestyle—Colossians 4:2 NLT.**
   "Devote yourselves to prayer with an alert mind and a thankful heart."

   According to this verse, how important should prayer be in your life?

   What attitude should accompany this type of prayer?

B. PRAYER IS DONE THROUGH OUR NEW COVENANT LENS

This section will be a little "theological," but it is essential to having a faith-filled prayer life. Effective prayer is done through our New Covenant lens. That means that we pray from the side of the finished work of the cross. Let's take a look.

1. **Hebrews 8:12-13**
   "'For I will be merciful to their unrighteousness, and their sins and their lawless deeds I will remember no more.' In that He says, 'A New Covenant,' He has made the first obsolete. Now what is becoming obsolete and growing old is ready to vanish away."

   Because of Jesus, what happens to your unrighteousness, sins, and lawless deeds?

   What type of covenant has God established for you?

   What happened to the Old Covenant?

   REVELATION DROP: Jesus has given us a New Covenant, and He made the old one obsolete. It's vanished! That's why we need to be mindful of our New Covenant reality and who we are in Christ when we read both the Old and New Testament scriptures. Let's look at this.

   Prayer Under the Old Covenant: Under the Old Covenant (Old Testament), the patriarchs talk to God about everything. Abraham intercedes for a city (Genesis 18:16-33); Isaac prays for his son Jacob and gives him the blessing (Genesis 27:27-29); Jacob prays for his family and generations to come (Genesis 48:14-15); Moses prays for God's manifested presence to go with him (Exodus 33:15-18); David prays and pours out his heart to the Lord on a regular basis as seen throughout the Psalms (e.g., Psalm 62:8); and Joshua, Hannah, Elijah, Jabez, Isaiah, Jeremiah, Daniel, and many other heroes of the Bible are people of prayer. Their prayers to God are heartfelt and include conversations, questions, requests, fellowship, and singing. They pray about their own private lives, their families, their nation, their calling, and God's purposes. Prayer is a not a cookie-cutter exercise under the Old Covenant; instead, it is the heart of man communicating with the heart of God.

Prayer Under the New Covenant: Under the New Covenant (New Testament), the early church and first believers talk to God about everything too! We see the disciples, the apostle Paul, church leaders, and everyday believers praying faith-filled prayers that God answers! They, too, pray about their spiritual lives, their families, the church, their calling, and God's will. Prayer should not be a rote, memorized experience for us as New Covenant (New Testament) believers; instead, we should always pray from our heart in light of our standing in Christ.

While we glean many things from the examples of those who prayed under the Old Covenant; as New Covenant believers, our prayer life has a different lens. The Lord made the Old Covenant obsolete and now, we get to pray from a different position—being raised up and seated with Christ—after His finished work on the cross. This is the lens from which we pray.

2.   **Hebrews 8:6**
"But now He has obtained a more excellent ministry, inasmuch as He is also Mediator of a better covenant, which was established on better promises."

Jesus is the Mediator of what kind of covenant?

What is this New Covenant established upon?

REVELATION DROP: Not only are we under a New Covenant with God, it's a new and better covenant based on better promises! How does that affect our prayer life? Let's look at an example of this.

A very well-known and well-loved prayer passage in the Bible is found in Psalm 51:10-11; David prays, *"Create in me a clean heart, O God, and renew a steadfast spirit within me. Do not cast me away from Your presence, and do not take Your Holy Spirit from me."* I love this passage, and I've sung many songs that revolve around this verse, but is this how a New Covenant believer in Christ should pray? At first glance, it seems like an amazing prayer that we should also pray; but let's break it down *technically* in light of our New Covenant lens.

"Create in me a clean heart, O God": Technically, when we received Jesus as Lord, God created and gave us a clean heart. We are 100 percent righteous in His eyes (2 Corinthians

5:17-21). So why would we pray for something we already have? We wouldn't! However, we may want to communicate this verse to the Lord in this way: *"Father, thank You that through Jesus You have given me a clean heart. You have made me righteous in Your sight. Create in me a continued desire to live from my heart in a manner that is fully pleasing to You."*

"Renew a steadfast spirit within me": Technically, this is a great thing to pray. In essence, you are asking the Lord to strengthen you and to help you with your perseverance and endurance. As followers of Christ, we all need that so you could pray this line as is.

"Do not cast me away from your presence": Technically, would the Lord cast you from His presence? No. Not if Hebrews 13:5 is true: *"For He Himself has said, "I will never leave you nor forsake you."* So, to pray this with a New Covenant lens, it might sound like this: *"Father, I am so thankful that You will never forsake me or cast me from Your presence. Lord, I want to experience more of Your presence and have a greater awareness that You are with me always."*

"Do not take Your Holy Spirit from me": Technically, would the Lord take the Holy Spirit from you? (In the Old Testament, the Holy Spirit does not dwell in the believers; He only comes upon them from time to time.) As New Covenant believers, Jesus tells us the Holy Spirit will live within us, and He comes upon us to give us power to be a witness for Christ. To pray this verse with the New Covenant lens might sound like this, *"Father, thank You for the Holy Spirit who lives within me. Help me to be more sensitive to His guidance, His voice, and His leadings. In Jesus' name amen."*

Can you see the importance of praying in light of our New Covenant lens?

C. PRAY IT OUT

What verse or passages stood out to you in this chapter? What truths stirred your heart?

Take a moment to pray and put these things into practice.

1. "Billy Graham Quotes." Brainy Quote, June 10, 2021, https://www.brainyquote.com/quotes/billy_graham_626385.

2. Stephen Nielsen, Basics of Prayer, (Morrisville: Lulu Press, 2013), 22.

CHAPTER 5:

THE "WHAT" OF PRAYER - PART 3

"Prayer is not trying to twist God's arm to make Him do something.
Prayer is receiving by faith what He has already done!"
Andrew Wommack

Prayer is a diverse subject. As it turns out, all prayer is not the same. As one of our mentors put it, in the same way that there are different kinds of sports, each with different equipment, goals, and rules; so, too, it is with prayer. There are different kinds of prayer, each with different equipment, goals, and rules. Our goal in prayer is to "pray by the rules." Let's look at the various types of prayer described in the Bible.

A. THERE ARE DIFFERENT TYPES OF PRAYER

Let's look at a partial list of the different types of prayer the Bible describes. Circle the words *ask, pray,* and *prayer* in each passage.

1.   **The Prayer of Petition (Request)—1 John 5:14-15**
   "Now this is the confidence that we have in Him, that if we ask anything according to His will, He hears us. And if we know that He hears us, whatever we ask, we know that we have the petitions that we have asked of Him."

   You can be certain God hears you when you pray in what way?

   If you know God hears you, what else can you be certain of?

   REVELATION DROP: The key to having our Prayer of Petition answered is to know that God heard our prayer. The difference between a prayer God *can hear* and one He *doesn't hear* is whether or not we are asking "according to His will." His will is found in His Word, so it turns out that God doesn't even hear our prayers if we're not praying according to His will.

   In other words, when we petition God, we don't ask Him if it is His will, rather we do our homework and pray from a position of knowing His will—as it is revealed in His Word. God wants to hear and answer our petitions, and He has made it easy for us to pray according to His will, because His Word is His will.

   So, if the secret to answered prayers is for God to hear them, then we want our prayers to be heard. If in order for God to hear our prayers, we must ask according to His will, then we need to know His will before we pray. If His will is His Word, then the more we know and pray His Word, the more effective our prayers will be! Kenneth E. Hagin puts it this way, *"The Bible, from Genesis to Revelation, is God's 'I Will' to every seeker for full salvation of spirit, soul, and body."*[1]

2. **The Prayer of Faith—Mark 11:24**
    "Therefore I say to you, whatever things you ask when you pray, believe that you receive them, and you will have them."

    What can you ask for?

    When you pray, what else are you supposed to do?

    If you believe you receive what you ask for when you pray, what will be the result?

    REVELATION DROP: Notice the two tenses in this verse: present tense and future tense. When we pray and ask the Father for things according to His will, we should believe we receive them (in the present tense) and we will have them (future tense.) When we pray the prayer of faith, we ask the Father for things that are according to His will (His Word), and at the same time we pray, we believe we receive what we've asked for. If, in the present, we believe we receive the things we asked for when we prayed, we will have them at some point, in the future. It could be one second after we believe we receive it, or it could be five years after we believe we receive it. The timing is in God's hands. Our job is to believe we receive what we ask for when we pray. Can you see that? This is a very important truth to understand; otherwise, we will be tempted to get discouraged or throw away our confidence if we do not get the things we prayed about within 24 hours.

3. **The Prayer of Supplication—Hebrews 5:7 AMPC**
    "In the days of His flesh [Jesus] offered up definite, special petitions [for that which He not only wanted but needed] and supplications with strong crying and tears to Him Who was [always] able to save Him [out] from death, and He was heard because of His reverence toward God [His godly fear, His piety]."

    What type of prayers did Jesus pray?

    What did the Father do?

    REVELATION DROP: Jesus offers up both the Prayer of Petition and the Prayer of Supplication. Both types of prayer are asking prayers, but one of them has more emotion and fervency to it. We can see that Jesus's Prayer of Petition includes definite, special requests for the things He wants and needs. His Prayer of Supplication is a pleading prayer with the emotions of strong crying and tears. Notice the distinction. Sometimes we pray and ask God for things without

44

emotion but purely on the basis of His Word; and at other times, there is an earnest, fervent, heartfelt pleading. Both types of prayer are necessary at different times for different things.

4. **The Prayer of Agreement—Matthew 18:19-20**

"Again I say to you that if two of you agree on earth concerning anything that they ask, it will be done for them by My Father in heaven. For where two or three are gathered together in My name, I am there in the midst of them."

How many people are needed for the Prayer of Agreement?

How would you describe *asking*?

How would you describe *agreement*?

If you do both of these things in prayer, of what can you be assured?

REVELATION DROP: The key to the Prayer of Agreement is that two or more people on earth ask the Father. It's not enough to just be on earth. It's not enough to just have two or more people. It's not enough to just agree. The secret is to put all of these things together and then do the most important thing—*ask!*

5. **The Prayer of Consecration—Matthew 26:36-39**

"Then Jesus came with them to a place called Gethsemane, and said to the disciples, 'Sit here while I go and pray over there.' And He took with Him Peter and the two sons of Zebedee, and He began to be sorrowful and deeply distressed. Then He said to them, 'My soul is exceedingly sorrowful, even to death. Stay here and watch with Me.' He went a little farther and fell on His face, and prayed, saying, 'O My Father, if it is possible, let this cup pass from Me; nevertheless, not as I will, but as You will.'"

What is the tone and spirit of this type of prayer?

What does "if it is possible, let this cup pass from Me" mean?

How does "nevertheless, not as I will, but as You will" mean?

REVELATION DROP: The Prayer of Consecration is a prayer of submitting our lives to God's plan. Jesus submits His will to the Father's will, and although He prays "if it is possible, let this cup pass from Me," He also consecrates Himself to God's purpose and adds "not as I will, but as You will." He surrenders Himself to God's higher plans.

When we don't know God's will (or we desire something different than His will), we can pray a Prayer of Consecration to submit to His will and purpose for our lives. In this type of prayer, we would add "not as I will, but as You will" to submit our life to God's plan.

However, when it comes to the Prayer of Petition, the Prayer of Faith or the Prayer of Agreement, we don't add the phrase "not as I will, but as You will" because when we know God's will as revealed in His Word, we are supposed to believe we receive it when we pray.

For example, if we are praying for God's wisdom, we know He has already promised to give His wisdom to anyone who asks for it (James 1:5). So, we pray the Prayer of Faith and ask God for His wisdom. We believe we receive it, and we trust God to give us His wisdom. There is no need to add but "not as I will, but as You will." Can you see that?

6. **The Prayer of Intercession—1 Timothy 2:1-4**
"Therefore I exhort first of all that supplications, prayers, intercessions, and giving of thanks be made for all men, for kings and all who are in authority, that we may lead a quiet and peaceable life in all godliness and reverence. For this is good and acceptable in the sight of God our Savior, who desires all men to be saved and to come to the knowledge of the truth."

What should you do "first of all"?

What should you pray for?

What is acceptable to God?

What does God desire?

REVELATION DROP: When we pray the Prayer of Intercession, we take the place of another in prayer; we stand between God and them. We pray for them in the way that we'd want someone to pray for us if we were them. We see an amazing example of intercession in Genesis 18 where Abraham intercedes for the people of Sodom. To do that, he stands between the Lord and the people of Sodom, and he prays for them as if he himself needs to be spared.

7. **The Prayer of Forgiveness—Mark 11:25**
"And whenever you stand praying, if you have anything against anyone, forgive him, that your Father in heaven may also forgive you your trespasses."

When you pray to your Father in heaven, what must you do to others on earth?

REVELATION DROP: It's a good practice to keep your heart free from offense by making a decision to forgive anyone of anything at all times. When you don't "feel" like forgiving others because of the hurt, disappointment, betrayal, abuse, or other pain they caused you, you can pray in the same way Jesus did when He was on the cross. Do you remember? He looked upon those who were crucifying Him and prayed, *"Father, forgive them" (Luke 23:34).* When you don't "feel" forgiveness for another, pray, "Father, forgive them." This will keep your heart free from unforgiveness and a root of bitterness and the Lord will help your feelings catch up eventually.

8.   **The Prayer of Thanksgiving—Philippians 4:6-7 AMPC**
       "Do not fret or have any anxiety about anything, but in every circumstance and in everything, by prayer and petition (definite requests), with thanksgiving, continue to make your wants known to God. And God's peace [shall be yours, that tranquil state of a soul assured of its salvation through Christ, and so fearing nothing from God and being content with its earthly lot of whatever sort that is, that peace] which transcends all understanding shall garrison and mount guard over your hearts and minds in Christ Jesus."

How much should you fret or be anxious?

What should you do in every circumstance and in everything?

What should accompany your prayers?

What has God promised?

REVELATION DROP: When we pray with definite requests and *with thanksgiving*, this displaces our anxiety and makes it possible to truly cast our cares on the Lord knowing He cares for us (1 Peter 5:7).

It turns out, God appreciates appreciation! Remember the story of the ten lepers who are cleansed (Luke 17:11-19)? Only one of the ten comes back to thank Jesus, and do you know what happens? That one leper is not only cleansed, but he receives the bonus of being made whole! The most courteous and faith-filled thing to do when someone blesses you is to say, *"Thank you."* How much more should we thank the Lord when we pray and believe He will grant our requests?

B.   THERE ARE DIFFERENT KINDS OF PRAYER EXPRESSIONS

We have all likely prayed prayers that didn't seem to make any difference. It may have seemed as if our prayers bounced off the ceiling and never made it to heaven at all. How can we pray prayers that make a difference?

1.   **Wait-on-the-Lord Prayer—Isaiah 40:31**
       "But those who wait on the LORD shall renew their strength; they shall mount up with wings like eagles, they shall run and not be weary, they shall walk and not faint."

What happens when you wait on the Lord?

How will you fly?

How will you run?

How will you walk?

How would you describe "waiting on the Lord"?

REVELATION DROP: One of the definitions of the word wait from Strong's Concordance is, *"a primitive root; to bind together (perhaps by twisting)."*[2] As we wait on the Lord in reading His Word, prayer, and quietly listening for the Spirit's impressions, we bind together with Him like a braid; and we receive His strength.

Second Corinthians 3:18 from the Passion Translation describes this same thing: *"We can all draw close to Him with the veil removed from our faces. And with no veil we all become like mirrors who brightly reflect the glory of the Lord Jesus. We are being transfigured into His very image as we move from one brighter level of glory to another. And this glorious transfiguration comes from the Lord, who is the Spirit."* When we spend time with the Lord beholding Him in the Word, we are transformed into His very same image—and strengthened to run, walk and fly!

2. **Earthshaking Prayer—Acts 4:31**
   "And when they had prayed, the place where they were assembled together was shaken; and they were all filled with the Holy Spirit, and they spoke the word of God with boldness."

What three things happened when this group of believers prayed?

REVELATION DROP: After being persecuted for their faith, the believers got together to pray! There was a passion and earnestness in their prayers. Rather than succumbing to a pity party, they went after God in prayer, and the results were literally earthshaking.

3. **Bold Prayer—Hebrews 4:16**
   "Let us therefore come boldly to the throne of grace, that we may obtain mercy and find grace to help in time of need."

In what way should you approach God's throne of grace?

What can you obtain in your time of need?

REVELATION DROP: You don't need to shrink back or feel any type of condemnation, inferiority, or shame when you pray, but rather because of Jesus, you can boldly approach your Father to obtain what you need. Think about children—do they have any reservations about boldly approaching their earthly father to ask for what they need? No. We can approach our Father with the same childlike faith and boldness because of Jesus!

Come boldly to His throne of grace! When our kids were little, I would wake up most mornings and run to God's throne of grace to receive a fresh dose of grace for my busy mom pace. As we were pioneering our church and trying to keep up with everything, I would often run to God's throne for a grace download! In recent seasons of transition, I continue to ask for more grace!

Do you need grace for your pace? Boldly run to His throne of grace to obtain mercy and a fresh grace deposit in your time of need.

4. **Hands-Lifted Prayer—1 Timothy 2:8**
"I desire therefore that the men pray everywhere, lifting up holy hands, without wrath and doubting."

Who should pray? (*Men* is reference to *mankind*, so this is for men and women.)

What bodily position is appropriate?

What heart position is necessary?

REVELATION DROP: The psalmist describes this type of prayer in Psalm 141:2: *"Let my prayer be set before You as incense, the lifting up of my hands as the evening sacrifice."* Our prayers and lifted hands are likened to incense—the incense we see in the Old Testament sacrifice (Exodus 30:6), as well as, the incense that ascends to the throne of God as described in the book of Revelation (Revelation 8:3,4).

The first time I saw someone lift their hands in prayer and worship, I was deeply touched. It was a Christian concert (something I had never been to before), and as I watched one of the lead singers lift her hands to the Lord to pray and sing, it was a beautiful visual of her surrender to the Lord and her personal connection with Him. Perhaps this type of prayer is new to you? If you have not yet lifted your hands to the Lord in prayer privately or in worship publicly, I encourage you to take a step of faith and do it.

5. **Kneeling Prayer—Ephesians 3:14**
"For this reason I bow my knees to the Father [of our Lord Jesus Christ, from whom the whole family in heaven and earth is named."

What does "bow my knees" in prayer represent?

To whom do you pray and bow your knee?

REVELATION DROP: Our posture in prayer can take on many forms, while we can pray standing, walking or sitting, there is something about kneeling that puts us in a humble and receptive position to talk to God.

6. **Loud, Tearful Prayer—Hebrews 5:7 NLT**
"While Jesus was here on earth, He offered prayers and pleadings, with a loud cry and tears, to the one who could rescue Him from death. And God heard His prayers because of His deep reverence for God."

What types of prayers does Jesus offer?

To whom does He pray?

Why does God hear His prayers?

What is the result?

REVELATION DROP: Sometimes our prayers are quiet, and that's okay; but they can also be loud. It's comforting to know the Lord cares for us, and we can empty our hearts out to the Lord. Are you facing a difficult or trying time? Maybe it's time to let your whole heart cry out to God in loud cries and tears.

7. **Desperate Prayer—2 Kings 20:1-7 NLT**
"About that time Hezekiah became deathly ill, and the prophet Isaiah son of Amoz went to visit him. He gave the king this message: 'This is what the LORD says: Set your affairs in order, for you are going to die. You will not recover from this illness.' When Hezekiah heard this, he turned his face to the wall and prayed to the LORD, 'Remember, O LORD, how I have always been faithful to You and have served You single-mindedly, always doing what pleases you.' Then he broke down and wept bitterly. But before Isaiah had left the middle courtyard, this message came to him from the LORD: 'Go back to Hezekiah, the leader of my people. Tell him, "This is what the LORD, the God of your ancestor David, says: I have heard your prayer and seen your tears. I will heal you, and three days from now you will get out of bed and go to the Temple of the LORD. I will add fifteen years to your life, and I will rescue you and this city from the king of Assyria. I will defend this city for my own honor and for the sake of my servant David."' Then Isaiah said, 'Make an ointment from figs.' So Hezekiah's servants spread the ointment over the boil, and Hezekiah recovered!"

What is Hezekiah's desperate situation?

What is the word of the Lord to Hezekiah?

Describe the way Hezekiah prayed and the words he said:

How does God answer?

REVELATION DROP: Are you at the end of your rope and feel like your back is against the wall? You are in good company; this is exactly how Hezekiah feels and God answers his desperate prayer! Notice, Hezekiah turns his face to the wall to pray. He cuts out all distractions and gets alone with God to pray earnest, heartfelt prayers. He isn't whining or begging, but he is earnest and praying with faith-filled tears—and God answers him.

8. **Fasting Prayer—Mark 9:23-29**

"Jesus said to him, 'If you can believe, all things are possible to him who believes.' Immediately the father of the child cried out and said with tears, 'Lord, I believe; help my unbelief!' When Jesus saw that the people came running together, He rebuked the unclean spirit, saying to it, 'Deaf and dumb spirit, I command you, come out of him and enter him no more!' Then the spirit cried out, convulsed him greatly, and came out of him. And he became as one dead, so that many said, "He is dead." But Jesus took him by the hand and lifted him up, and he arose. And when He had come into the house, His disciples asked Him privately, 'Why could we not cast it out?' So He said to them, 'This kind can come out by nothing but prayer and fasting.'"

What is the first thing Jesus says?

What is the man's response to Jesus?

What do the disciples ask Jesus?

How does Jesus respond?

REVELATION DROP: As we discussed earlier, fasting and prayer are important, but perhaps not for the reasons you think. When we fast and pray, we are not twisting God's arm to answer us. God is not more inclined to answer our prayers if we fast longer. There is a role for fasting, but it has to do with our faith, not God's willingness to answer our prayers.

In this story, Jesus casts a deaf and dumb spirit out of a young boy. When Jesus says, *"This kind can come out by nothing but prayer and fasting,"* He is referring to unbelief, not to the deaf and dumb spirit. Unbelief goes when we fast and pray—prayer and fasting quiets our flesh so that our spirit rises up in faith to believe God.

When we fast and pray, we are not doing sacrificial penance to persuade God to deliver us; nor are we trying to convince the devil to leave us alone. Rather, when we fast and pray, we are subduing our flesh and allowing our spirit to become more sensitive to the things of God. As our

51

spirit is more dominant, unbelief goes. It is faith that casts out demons, not prayer and fasting; but prayer and fasting helps unbelief to go so that faith can operate. Can you see that?

So what's the bottom line? *Don't fast and pray* to convince God to do something for you, but rather *do fast and pray* to quiet your flesh, increase your spiritual sensitivity, and build your faith in God's Word.

9.   **Humble Prayer—2 Chronicles 7:14**
       "If My people who are called by My name will humble themselves, and pray and seek My face, and turn from their wicked ways, then I will hear from heaven, and will forgive their sin and heal their land."

What should God's people do?

What disposition should we have?

What will God do?

10.   **Fervent Prayer—James 5:16**
       "The effective, fervent prayer of a righteous man avails much."

What kind of prayer is effective and avails much?

REVELATION DROP: Fervent prayer is the kind of prayer that gets the job done. It's the kind of prayer that doesn't give up. By definition, according to Strong's Concordance, the Greek word translated as *fervent* is *energeo*, and its meanings include *"to be operative, be at work, put forth power,"*[3] as well as, *"energize, working in a situation which brings it from one stage (point) to the next, like an electrical current energizing a wire, bringing it to a shining light-bulb."*[4] Don't bore God (or yourself!) with mealy mouthed prayers—pray energized prayers that get God's attention and produce results.

C.   PRAY IT OUT

What verse or passages stood out to you in this chapter? What truths stirred your heart?

Take a moment to pray and put these things into practice.

1.   "Kenneth E. Hagin Quotes," AZ Quotes, May 7, 2021, https://www.azquotes.com/author/46187-Kenneth_E_Hagin.

2.   Blue Letter Bible, s.v. "H7965 - šālôm," May 8, 2021, https://www.blueletterbible.org//lang/lexicon/lexicon.cfm?Strongs=H7965&t=KJV.

3.   Blue Letter Bible, s.v. "G1754 - energeō," April 18, 2021. https://www.blueletterbible.org//lang/lexicon/lexicon.cfm?Strongs=G1754&t=KJV.

4.   Bible Hub, s.v. "1754 Energeo," March 22, 2021, https://biblehub.com/greek/1754.htm.

SECTION 3:

THE "WHO" OF PRAYER

CHAPTER 6:

THE "WHO" OF PRAYER - PART 1

"If you are a stranger to prayer, you are a stranger to the greatest source of power known to human beings."
Billy Sunday

To whom do we pray? This is the big question! All effective prayer starts and originates with God.

Our loving heavenly Father is the all-powerful (omnipotent), all-knowing (omniscient), and ever-present (omnipresent) God. He is the Almighty, miracle-working God. He is the source of all wisdom and provision. He is the author and the finisher, the Alpha and the Omega, the Beginning and the End. Everything comes from, by, and through Him. He is the Creator of the ends of the Earth—the Most High God. Above Him there is no other! And to think that we can approach Him through the mighty name of Jesus. What a privilege!

Let's dig a little deep on the "who" of prayer.

A. WE PRAY TO THE FATHER—IN JESUS' NAME

When it comes to prayer, there is often confusion on where we direct our prayers. Do we pray to God Almighty? To Jesus? Do we pray to the Holy Spirit? To whom do we pray? While prayer is not "mechanical"; we should "pray by the rules" God has given us. Thankfully, Jesus gave us very clear directions. He taught us to pray to God the Father, in Jesus's Name and by the power of the Holy Spirit!

1.   **John 16:23-24**

"And in that day you will ask Me nothing. Most assuredly, I say to you, whatever you ask the Father in My name He will give you. Until now you have asked nothing in My name. Ask, and you will receive, that your joy may be full."

In that day (after the resurrection), who does Jesus say *you would not address* in prayer?

Who does Jesus say *you should address* in prayers?

In whose name are you authorized to pray?

What result does the Lord want you to experience?

REVELATION DROP: We looked at this previously, but it's good to remember that we pray to the Father in Jesus's Name. You will notice that the disciples never prayed to Jesus (but they did have numerous conversations with Him), and nowhere in the Bible are we told to pray to the Holy Spirit (yet we can have communion with Him). We are told to pray to the Father. So then, if our prayers and requests should be directed to our heavenly Father, in what ways should we communicate with Jesus and the Holy Spirit?

Here's a good rule of thumb:

>> **Pray to your heavenly Father:** We pray to the Father in Jesus's Name, and we can ask, require, call for, and request anything from Him according to His will.

>> **Talk to the Lord Jesus:** We don't pray to Jesus, but we can talk to Jesus. Just as the disciples did not pray to Jesus but talked, traveled, observed, leaned on, and learned from Him, so, too, can we.

>> **Commune with the Holy Spirit:** We don't pray to the Holy Spirit, but we do talk and commune with Him. He lives within us, and we can have fellowship with Him. We can always listen to His still small voice—His guidance and His witness to the truth.

We pray to the Father in Jesus's name by the power of the Spirit.

I love how 2 Corinthians 13:14 NLT describes the way we can relate to God the Father, Jesus our lord, and the Holy Spirit: *"May the grace of the Lord Jesus Christ, the love of God, and the fellowship of the Holy Spirit be with you all."*

2. **John 16:26-27**
"In that day you will ask in My name, and I do not say to you that I shall pray the Father for you; for the Father Himself loves you, because you have loved Me, and have believed that I came forth from God."

Who loves you?

What does the Father love about you?

B. WE PRAY TO THE FATHER—WHO HEARS OUR PRAYERS

1. **1 John 5:14-15**
"Now this is the confidence that we have in Him, that if we ask anything according to His will, He hears us. And if we know that He hears us, whatever we ask, we know that we have the petitions that we have asked of Him."

What is one way you can be certain God hears your prayers?

If you know He hears your prayers, what else do you know?

REVELATION DROP: How do we know we are praying according to God's will? Anytime we pray according to God's Word, we know it is His will, and we know He hears us. That's one reason praying the Scriptures is a good practice.

2.   **Psalm 34:4-6**
"I sought the LORD, and He heard me, and delivered me from all my fears. They looked to Him and were radiant, and their faces were not ashamed. This poor man cried out, and the LORD heard him, and saved him out of all his troubles."

When you *seek the Lord*, what are you promised?

When you *look to the Lord*, what is the result?

When you *cry out to the Lord*, what does God promise?

C.   WE PRAY TO THE FATHER—WHO WANTS TO BLESS US

1.   **Ephesians 1:2-3**
"Grace to you and peace from God our Father and the Lord Jesus Christ. Blessed be the God and Father of our Lord Jesus Christ, who has blessed us with every spiritual blessing in the heavenly places in Christ."

What has God already blessed you with?

Where are these blessings located?

What do you think is included in "every spiritual blessing"?

REVELATION DROP: God is not a withholder; He is a giver, and He loves to bless His children. In fact, God blessed you with every spiritual blessing in heaven before you even knew you needed them! Since everything in life is spiritual—whether in relationship with the Lord, in health, in finances, in relationships with others, or in purpose—all the blessings we need to live life have already been given to us through our relationship with Jesus! In prayer, we are not pleading with God to bless us; we are agreeing with Him and what He's already stated. Because we are "in Christ," we can simply ask and put in our request to receive the heavenly blessings He's already bought and paid for.

2. **Psalm 84:11**

"For the LORD God is a sun and shield; the LORD will give grace and glory; no good thing will He withhold from those who walk uprightly."

What does the Lord give?

What does the Lord not withhold?

REVELATION DROP: It's easy to read passages like this about the blessings for the "upright" and the "righteous" and then to disqualify ourselves because we know our own faults. But the truth is that no one is upright enough or righteous enough to receive any of God's blessings. The only Person who is blemish free, perfect, upright, or righteous is Jesus Christ. Thankfully, Jesus didn't keep this status to Himself; instead, when we received and confessed Him as our Lord, He gave us His upright standing, and He made us perfectly righteous—just as righteous as Himself (2 Corinthians 5:21). This free gift of righteousness changes everything and gives us the privilege of approaching our heavenly Father with boldness to access all of His blessings (Hebrews 4:16).

3. **1 John 4:17**

"Love has been perfected among us in this: that we may have boldness in the day of judgment; because as He is, so are we in this world."

What does God want you to have in "the day of judgment"?

How are you in this world?

REVELATION DROP: We often relegate this passage to the future "judgment to come," but there is a present tense application we don't want to miss. Notice, it says **"As He (Jesus) is, so are we in this world!"** This is a big revelation. God doesn't see us as we are; He sees us as He sees Jesus—now! Jesus never deals with guilt, inferiority, or a sense of unworthiness. Jesus can ask the Father for anything and the Father grants His request. Jesus is victorious and seated in victory. God wants us to see ourselves seated "in Christ"—He wants us to live in the reality that just as Jesus is, so are we in this world. We are just as upright, righteous, victorious, healed, and blessed as Jesus. When we know and believe this truth, it's easy to pray with boldness. This is a huge revelation, and I hope you will meditate upon this.

D. WE PRAY TO THE FATHER—WHO WANTS TO ANSWER

1. **Jeremiah 33:3**

"Call to Me, and I will answer you, and show you great and mighty things, which you do not know."

What does God want you to do?

What has He promised to do?

What happens if you do not "call to" Him?

2.   **Matthew 7:7-11**
        "Ask, and it will be given to you; seek, and you will find; knock, and it will be opened to you. For everyone who asks receives, and he who seeks finds, and to him who knocks it will be opened. Or what man is there among you who, if his son asks for bread, will give him a stone? Or if he asks for a fish, will he give him a serpent? If you then, being evil, know how to give good gifts to your children, how much more will your Father who is in heaven give good things to those who ask Him!"

        What does He promise to do in response to your *asking*, *seeking*, and *knocking*?

        In the last line, what does our Father promise?

        REVELATION DROP: If an earthly father wants to bless his children, how much more does our heavenly Father want to bless us with good things? E.M. Bounds explains this passage so eloquently, *"Prayer is asking, seeking, and knocking at the door for something we have not, which we desire, and which God has promised to us . . . Prayer is the voice of need crying out to Him who is inexhaustible in resources. Prayer is helplessness reposing with childlike confidence on the world of its Father in heaven."*[1]

3.   **Mark 11:24**
        "Therefore I say to you, whatever things you ask when you pray, believe that you receive them, and you will have them."

        When you pray, what are you to believe?

        When should you believe?

        What has Jesus promised?

4.   **Habakkuk 2:1-2**
        "I will stand my watch and set myself on the rampart, and watch to see what He will say to me, and what I will answer when I am corrected. Then the LORD answered me and said: 'Write the vision and make it plain on tablets, that he may run who reads it.'"

        a.   **Verse 1: "stand my watch"**
                When the prophet Habakkuk states that he will "stand his watch and set himself on the

rampart," this is a picture of getting into a proactive position of watching in prayer—that is, being quiet, still, discerning and ready to hear.

How do you "stand your watch" and get quiet, still, and ready to hear from God?

b. **Verse 1: "watch to see"**
Habakkuk opens his heart to what God wants to show him. He tunes his spirit into the Holy Spirit to see what revelation, thoughts, visions, dreams, or witty ideas the Lord impresses upon him.

How do you "watch to see" what the Lord wants to show you?

REVELATION DROP: Mark Virkler, in his book *4 Keys to Hearing God's Voice*, outlines this entire passage and the dialogue of prayer in Habakkuk. He describes the challenge of being both rational and logical while also spiritual:

"Being a logical, rational person, observable facts that could be verified by my physical senses were the foundations of my life, including my spiritual life. I had never thought of opening the eyes of my heart and looking for vision. However, I have come to believe that this is exactly what God wants me to do. He gave me eyes in my heart to see in the spirit the vision and movement of Almighty God. There is an active spirit world all around us, full of angels, demons, the Holy Spirit, the omnipresent Father, and His omnipresent Son, Jesus. The only reasons for me not to see this reality are unbelief or lack of knowledge. . . . In order to see, we must look. Daniel saw a vision in his mind and said, "I was looking . . . I kept looking . . . I kept looking" (Daniel 7:2,9,13). As I pray, I look for Jesus, and I watch as He speaks to me, doing and saying the things that are on His heart. Many Christians will find that if they will only look, they will see. Jesus is Emmanuel, God with us (Matthew 1:23). It is as simple as that. You can see Christ present with you because Christ is present with you. In fact, the vision may come so easily that you will be tempted to reject it, thinking it is just you."[2]

c. **Verse 1: "what He will say to me"**
As you listen to the Lord in prayer, (remember it's a dialogue, not a monologue) He will speak to your heart with answers, direction, and insight.

In recent times, what have you sensed the Lord speaking to your heart as you pray?

What words, ideas, thoughts, revelation, dreams, vision, images, or witty ideas has He shown you lately? Describe it.

REVELATION DROP: I will never forget an occasion when this truth dawned on me. I was newly married, kneeling by my couch and praying about a particular job offer I had received. The job was to be the Student Activities Director for a Christian college. As I was asking the Lord, "Father, is this the right job? Do You want me to take it?" I found myself suddenly "daydreaming" about the first activity I would lead if I took the job. I envisioned a huge anniversary picnic for the ministry complete with 3-on-3 basketball games, a softball game, activities for kids, and a giant cake to serve the 2,000 people who would attend this event. I could see the whole thing in detail. As I was praying and envisioning all of these things, I said, "I'm sorry, Lord. I am getting distracted! I really want to know; do You want me to take this job?" And then it hit me. God was answering my prayer in real time—the "what He will say to me" was evidenced by Him dropping all kinds of creative ideas into my heart for this very job. Well, needless to say, I took the job, and the first event I oversaw was the anniversary picnic with all of these details.

d. **Verse 2: "Write the vision"**
Writing down the things the Lord shows us and those things He speaks to our heart is essential. When we can see the vision, it's easy to run with it.

Have you ever journaled, recorded, or drawn in picture form the things God speaks to you? If so, describe it. If not, perhaps this is a good time to do it.

REVELATION DROP: Writing down your prayer dialogues is a great practice to develop! Early in my Christian life, I wrote my prayers in a journal; this was the beginning of cultivating a lifetime of prayer journals with the Lord. Each night I would write my prayers to the Lord. They were a combination of thanking the Lord and appreciating His presence in my life, as well as, a log of specific requests I asked of Him.

When my husband and I were first married and as we prayed about our future, the Lord began to show us internal images and pictures of the things He desired for us. We saw ourselves with four kids. We saw ourselves leading some type of ministry. We saw ourselves traveling overseas to preach the Word. We saw ourselves enjoying one another and being fit. We took time to "write the vision" and made a stick-figure drawing of all of these things along with several scriptures we added to the drawing. It was not sophisticated at all. It was very simple, and yet it was a vision we could run with. Well, here we are over 35 years later, and the Lord has brought to pass every single thing we drew on that piece of paper. If you haven't gotten into the practice of journaling yet, I encourage you to do so.

E. PRAY IT OUT

What verse or passages stood out to you in this chapter? What truths stirred your heart?

Take a moment to pray and put these things into practice.

1. E. M. Bounds, Possibilities of Prayer, (Grand Rapids: Baker Book House, 1979), 41, 129.
2. "Four Keys to Hearing God's Voice," Communion With God Ministries, March 23, 2021, https://www.cwgministries.org/Four-Keys-to-Hearing-Gods-Voice.

CHAPTER 7:

THE "WHO" OF PRAYER - PART 2

"The Christian should work as if all depended upon him,
and pray as if it all depended upon God."
Charles Spurgeon

Who prays? You do! Prayer is a verb. In order to be an effective *pray-er,* you, the believer, must pray. God is the One to whom we pray, and He alone is the One who answers prayer; but *we* are the ones who must do the praying.

Martin Luther said, *"To be a Christian without prayer is no more possible than to be alive without breathing."*[1] This is so true. I cannot think of anything that has enriched, accelerated, and deepened my own relationship with the Lord more than prayer.

Prayer is a privilege for believers. It is your lifeline to heaven. It's the primary way believers contact God, and there is both the personal side and the business side of prayer. As we've mentioned, through prayer you can develop your fellowship with the Lord, you can make requests of the Lord, and you can produce fruit for the Lord. Sometimes our prayer life is very personal, and at other times, we are taking care of kingdom business.

I once heard my friend Patsy Cameneti (author of *For Such a Time As This* and someone from whom I've learned so much about prayer) talk about cultivating your *personal relationship* and your *business relationship* with God through prayer. The idea is that as you spend *personal time* with God pouring out your heart in prayer, He will work in you and minister things to you personally. When you spend *business time* with God, it's as if you are partnering with God and sitting in Heaven's board room "busy about your Father's business." As you pray about the advancement of His Church, He will give believers insights, wisdom, ability, and heavenly strategies to spread the gospel, to encourage others, and to build His Church.

Cultivating our *personal relationship* through alone time with God is vital for developing intimacy with the Lord and crucial for the flow of God's life into ours. Developing our *business relationship* with God by praying for His will to be done on earth is exciting and essential for developing eternal fruit.

A.   PRAYER IS A PRIVILEGE FOR BELIEVERS

Prayer is a privilege reserved for believers. Just as children are able to approach their earthly fathers with confidence and boldness, so, too, as God's children, we have been given the privilege of approaching Him.

1.   **John 1:10-12**
"He was in the world, and the world was made through Him, and the world did not know Him.

He came to His own, and His own did not receive Him. But as many as received Him, to them He gave the right to become children of God, to those who believe in His name: who were born, not of blood, nor of the will of the flesh, nor of the will of man, but of God."

Who does not know Him (Jesus)?

Jesus gave the right to "become children of God" to whom?

Those who receive Jesus and believe in His name are born of whom?

REVELATION DROP: While God is the Creator of all things, He is the Father only of those who "receive and believe" in Jesus. Those who believe and receive Jesus are the ones who are "born of God," also called being born-again (John 3). When you become a child of God, through receiving and believing in Jesus, you also receive the privilege of access to the Father and the freedom to pray bold prayers.

2.   **Psalm 66:16-19 NLT**
"Come and listen, all you who fear God, and I will tell you what He did for me. For I cried out to Him for help, praising Him as I spoke. If I had not confessed the sin in my heart, the Lord would not have listened. But God did listen! He paid attention to my prayer. Praise God, who did not ignore my prayer or withdraw His unfailing love from me."

What happens to the person who has not confessed their sin and received the Lord?

What happens to the person who confesses their sin and receives Jesus as Lord?

3.   **John 9:31**
"Now we know that God does not hear sinners; but if anyone is a worshiper of God and does His will, He hears him."

Who does God not hear?

Who does God hear?

REVELATION DROP: If you are a born-again believer in Jesus, God does not see you as a sinner "in sin"; instead, He sees you as His child "in Christ"—just as righteous as Jesus—and He hears you. The good news is that all of God's children are equally able to pray. God doesn't hear the prayers of one of His children more than another. He doesn't hear the preacher's prayers more than yours. He has leveled the "praying field" for all of us! He hears the faith-filled prayers of all of His children.

You might wonder about God's willingness to answer the prayers of someone who is not yet a believer? Perhaps, He answered your prayers before you came to Christ and you wonder how that factors in? Interestingly, it seems that at times God works in our lives, answers prayer and rescues us "on credit" knowing that we will come to Christ eventually.

We see an example of this in Acts 10 with a man named Cornelius. *"In Caesarea there lived a Roman army officer named Cornelius, who was a captain of the Italian Regiment. He was a devout, God-fearing man, as was everyone in his household. He gave generously to the poor and prayed regularly to God. One afternoon about three o'clock, he had a vision in which he saw an angel of God coming toward him. "Cornelius!" the angel said. Cornelius stared at him in terror. "What is it, sir?" he asked the angel. And the angel replied, "Your prayers and gifts to the poor have been received by God as an offering!"* (Acts 10:1-4 NLT) The Bible tells us that Cornelius was a Roman soldier who prayed, worshipped God and gave generously to help the poor—as a result "his name came up" before the Lord and God did a wonderful work in bringing the gospel to him through Peter and this led to he and his entire family coming to Christ!

4.   **1 John 3:21-22**

"Beloved, if our heart does not condemn us, we have confidence toward God. And whatever we ask we receive from Him, because we keep His commandments and do those things that are pleasing in His sight."

What allows you to have confidence before God?

When you have confidence before God, what does this allow you to do?

B. PRAYER IS A PERSONAL EXPERIENCE FOR BELIEVERS

One of the very best lifestyles you can develop as a Christian is to be a person of prayer. Developing your daily habit of personal prayer life with God will give you an intimate relationship with the Lord. Some people call this their "quiet time" or "daily prayer time." This is a specific time set aside and reserved for the Lord, and it can include reading your Bible, worshiping Him, pouring out your heart to Him, praying in the Spirit, and making specific requests. It is during these prayer times with God that He will imprint so many wonderful things on your heart and impart life-changing direction, truth, wisdom, and insight to your mind and spirit.

Praying is very intentional, but it is not a duty or a mechanical religious obligation; rather, it's the pursuit of God. It's the privilege of seeking God and communing with our creator. Within all of us there is a divine itch that can only be scratched by connecting with God in a heartfelt way.

Let's look at the *personal* side of prayer first and then we will look at the *business* partnership we can have with the Lord in prayer.

1.   **Pray and talk to the Lord—Psalm 27:7-8 NLT.**
"Hear me as I pray, O Lord. Be merciful and answer me! My heart has heard you say, 'Come and talk with me.' And my heart responds, 'Lord, I am coming.'"

What does the Lord want you to do?

What is your response to Him?

2. **Pray and sincerely seek the Lord—Hebrews 11:6 NLT.**
"And it is impossible to please God without faith. Anyone who wants to come to Him must believe that God exists and that He rewards those who sincerely seek Him."

What is impossible to do without faith?

In order to come to God, what do you have to believe?

What does God do for those who sincerely seek Him?

3. **Pray with your whole heart—Jeremiah 29:11-14.**
"For I know the thoughts that I think toward you, says the LORD, thoughts of peace and not of evil, to give you a future and a hope. Then you will call upon Me and go and pray to Me, and I will listen to you. And you will seek Me and find Me, when you search for Me with all your heart. I will be found by you, says the LORD."

What type of thoughts does God think toward you?

What does God promise when you call upon Him and pray to Him?

What kind of people does the Lord say will find Him?

4. **Pray and talk to God in a private place—Matthew 6:5-6.**
"And when you pray, you shall not be like the hypocrites. For they love to pray standing in the synagogues and on the corners of the streets, that they may be seen by men. Assuredly, I say to you, they have their reward. But you, when you pray, go into your room, and when you have shut your door, pray to your Father who is in the secret place; and your Father who sees in secret will reward you openly."

Who sees you when you pray in your secret place?

What has God promised?

5. **Pray and talk to God alone—Mark 1:35.**

"Now in the morning, having risen a long while before daylight, He went out and departed to a solitary place; and there He prayed."

What does this passage tell you about the "who," "where," and "when" of Jesus' private prayer life with God?

6. **Pray and talk to God first—Psalm 5:1-3.**

"Give ear to my words, O LORD, consider my meditation. Give heed to the voice of my cry, my King and my God, for to You I will pray. My voice You shall hear in the morning, O LORD; in the morning I will direct it to You, and I will look up."

In this passage on prayer, describe the morning attitude and expectation of the psalmist:

Why do you think praying in the morning is a good idea?

7. **Pray and sing songs to God—Ephesians 5:18-20 NLT.**

"...be filled with the Holy Spirit, singing psalms and hymns and spiritual songs among your-selves, and making music to the Lord in your hearts. And give thanks for everything to God the Father in the name of our Lord Jesus Christ."

What are psalms, hymns and spiritual songs?

Who do you sing and make music to?

REVELATION DROP: Have you ever allowed your heart to pray and sing whatever words filled your heart? It's such a great way to spend time with the Lord. Simply start by praying and singing in the spirit—then sing out whatever words or melody He puts in your heart.

8. **Pray when you are in trouble—Psalm 34:4-6 NLT.**

"I prayed to the Lord, and he answered me. He freed me from all my fears. Those who look to him for help will be radiant with joy; no shadow of shame will darken their faces. In my desper-ation I prayed, and the Lord listened; he saved me from all my troubles."

When can you pray?

How will God respond?

9. **Pray and talk to God always—1 Thessalonians 5:17.**
"Pray without ceasing."

How are you supposed to pray?

REVELATION DROP: You might wonder how someone could "pray without ceasing." After all, don't you have to eat, work, study, and sleep? Of course, you do! Brother Andrew Murray is famously known for encouraging people to "practice His Presence" at all times. You can "pray without ceasing" while brushing your teeth, making breakfast, driving in your car, walking to an important meeting, and while shopping, fixing dinner, doing homework, or mowing the lawn. This 24/7 awareness and two-way communication between you and the Lord is vital. I like to think of it as constantly having our "spiritual radar" on and keeping our "spiritual WIFI" turned on all day. When we pray this way, we can "pick up" the Lord's notifications and promptings on the "radar screen" of our heart, and we can send messages via prayer back to His radar screen throughout the day.

C. PRAYER IS A BUSINESS PARTNERSHIP FOR BELIEVERS

1. **Pray intentionally and be busy about the Father's business—Luke 2:41-49.**
"His parents went to Jerusalem every year at the Feast of the Passover. And when He was twelve years old, they went up to Jerusalem according to the custom of the feast. When they had finished the days, as they returned, the Boy Jesus lingered behind in Jerusalem. And Joseph and His mother did not know it; but supposing Him to have been in the company, they went a day's journey, and sought Him among their relatives and acquaintances. So when they did not find Him, they returned to Jerusalem, seeking Him. Now so it was that after three days they found Him in the temple, sitting in the midst of the teachers, both listening to them and asking them questions. And all who heard Him were astonished at His understanding and answers. So when they saw Him, they were amazed; and His mother said to Him, 'Son, why have You done this to us? Look, Your father and I have sought You anxiously.' And He said to them, 'Why did you seek Me? Did you not know that I must be about My Father's business?'"

What do Jesus' parents find Him doing?

How do the religious leaders respond to His wisdom?

What does Jesus say He must do?

REVELATION DROP: Jesus had a very *personal* relationship with His Father and yet we also see His devotion to the *business* side of His relationship. Jesus is only twelve years old in this passage, yet already it is easy to see His wisdom around the things of God. Throughout His life, He was busy about His Father's business by preaching the Gospel to the lost, showing compassion and healing the sick, equipping His disciples to proclaim His Word, and leading people into the abundant life He had come to give them.

2. **Pray with compassion for laborers to go into the harvest—Matthew 9:35-38.**

   "Then Jesus went about all the cities and villages, teaching in their synagogues, preaching the gospel of the kingdom, and healing every sickness and every disease among the people. But when He saw the multitudes, He was moved with compassion for them, because they were weary and scattered, like sheep having no shepherd. Then He said to His disciples, 'The harvest truly is plentiful, but the laborers are few. Therefore pray the Lord of the harvest to send out laborers into His harvest.'"

   What does Jesus see as He goes about the Father's business of teaching, preaching and healing?

   What does Jesus say to His disciples?

   What does Jesus say to pray?

3. **Pray earnestly for preachers to speak the Word—Colossians 4:2-4.**

   "Continue earnestly in prayer, being vigilant in it with thanksgiving; meanwhile praying also for us, that God would open to us a door for the word, to speak the mystery of Christ, for which I am also in chains, that I may make it manifest, as I ought to speak."

   What type of prayers does the Apostle Paul request for carrying on the "business" of ministry?

4. **Pray with passion for the health and prosperity of God's people—3 John 2.**

   "Beloved, I pray that you may prosper in all things and be in health, just as your soul prospers."

   What should we pray for when it comes to the general prosperity of others (spiritually)?

   What should we pray for when it comes to their health (physically)?

   What should we pray for when it comes to their soul (mentally and emotionally)?

REVELATION DROP: Have you prayed for health and prosperity lately? Often these things are labeled as the "health and wealth" gospel and they get a bad reputation. That is so unfortunate since these truths are taught throughout the Bible. In fact, God's Word goes so far as to tell us, *"Let the LORD be magnified, Who has pleasure in the prosperity of His servant"* (Psalm 35:27). Did you know when mentioned in the Bible, the word *prosperity* is from the word *shalom*? It means "completeness, soundness, welfare, peace."[2] Psalm 103 tells us to, *"Bless the Lord, O my soul; and all that is within me, bless His holy name! Bless the Lord, O my soul, and forget not all His benefits: Who forgives all your iniquities, Who heals all your diseases."* Notice health and wealth is directly connected to the health and prosperity of our souls. When we pray for ourselves or others, let's pray for wholistic health and prosperity in spirit, soul, and body.

Can you see the wonderful privilege believers have when it comes to prayer? The *personal* side of time with the Lord is always rewarding and fulfilling, while the *business* side of time with the Lord has a different kingdom-minded fulfilment and the satisfaction of furthering His cause.

D.   PRAY IT OUT

What verse or passages stood out to you in this chapter? What truths stirred your heart?

Take a moment to pray and put these things into practice.

1. "Martin Luther Quotes." Brainy Quote, March 13, 2021, https://www.brainyquote.com/quotes/martin_luther_385793.

2. Blue Letter Bible, s.v. "šālôm," June 1, 2021, https://www.blueletterbible.org/lexicon/h7965/kjv/wlc/0-1/.

CHAPTER 8

THE "WHO" OF PRAYER - PART 3

"Pray without ceasing on behalf of everyone.
For in them there is hope of repentance so that they may attain to God.
Permit them, then, to be instructed by your works, if in no other way.
Be meek in response to their wrath, humble in opposition to their boasting;
to their blasphemies return your prayers; in contrast to their error be steadfast in the faith;
and for their cruelty display your gentleness."
Ignatius, c. A.D. 110

When it comes to prayer, for whom do we pray? Ourselves? Should we pray for unbelievers? Our enemies? Our church? Our leaders? Yes, and yes!

We can and should pray for ourselves and others—both other believers and non-believers. Not only can we pray for others, we can pray with others. Let's look at this.

A.   PRAY FOR YOURSELF

Is it selfish to pray for yourself? Absolutely not! Jesus gave us numerous words of encouragement to pray faith-filled prayers for ourselves and others. After all, who cares more about your life than you? While others may pray for you, you shouldn't expect others to do your praying. Don't abdicate your own responsibility to pray for yourself. You pray for you. The Bible is loaded with all kinds of promises and assurances to help you pray for your own needs and desires. Let's look at a couple of passages to get you started.

1.   **Pray for the wisdom you need—James 1:5-6.**
     "If any of you lacks wisdom, let him ask of God, who gives to all liberally and without reproach, and it will be given to him. But let him ask in faith, with no doubting, for he who doubts is like a wave of the sea driven and tossed by the wind."

     If you pray for wisdom, of what can you be certain?

     In what way should you ask for wisdom?

2.   **Pray and your joy will be full—John 16:23-24.**
     "Most assuredly, I say to you, whatever you ask the Father in My name He will give you. Until now you have asked nothing in My name. Ask, and you will receive, that your joy may be full."

What can you ask the Father for in Jesus' name?

What will He do?

What result does He want for you?

3. **Pray and believe you receive—Mark 11:24 NLT.**
    "Therefore I say to you, whatever things you ask when you pray, believe that you receive them, and you will have them."

What can you ask when you pray?

What should you do when you pray?

What should you believe?

What will result?

REVELATION DROP: There are many keywords in this passage which we looked at earlier, and we will look at again, later in the book, but right now I want to draw your attention to the word *receive*. That interesting word is the Greek word *lambano*, and according to *Strong's Concordance*, its meanings include: "to take, to have, to take hold of, to claim, etc."[1] This is a verb. It's not a passive word but rather an active word. That means without apology, by faith, we can "take, claim, and have" the things we have prayed and believed we received.

4. **Pray when you are mistreated—Psalm 109:4.**
    "In return for my love they are my accusers, But I give myself to prayer."

What should we do when we are facing challenges, being mistreated and misunderstood?

REVELATION DROP: David, the psalmist, knew the secret to living life God's way—prayer! When his enemies betrayed his love by accusing him and mistreating him, he didn't give in to bitterness, self-pity or returning hatred. Instead, he gave himself to prayer.

B. PRAY FOR OTHERS

Everyone needs and desires prayer.

1. **Pray for others with joy—Philippians 1:4 NLT.**
   "Whenever I pray, I make my requests for all of you with joy."

   How are you to pray and make requests?

2. **Pray for kings, presidents, and authorities—1 Timothy 2:1-4.**
   "Therefore I exhort first of all that supplications, prayers, intercessions, and giving of thanks be made for all men, for kings and all who are in authority, that we may lead a quiet and peaceable life in all godliness and reverence. For this is good and acceptable in the sight of God our Savior, who desires all men to be saved and to come to the knowledge of the truth."

   What leaders should you pray for first?

   Why are you called to pray for those in authority?

   Write down the name of the authorities you should be praying for.

3. **Pray for believers.**
   Praying for one another is essential. Let's look at ways to pray for believers.

   a. **Colossians 1:3-4**
       "We give thanks to the God and Father of our Lord Jesus Christ, praying always for you, since we heard of your faith in Christ Jesus and of your love for all the saints."

       For whom should you give thanks and prayer?

   b. **Colossians 4:12**
       "Epaphras, who is one of you, a bondservant of Christ, greets you, always laboring fervently for you in prayers, that you may stand perfect and complete in all the will of God."

       How does Epaphras pray?

       What does he pray for the believers?

       REVELATION DROP: I think this is one of the best ways to pray for people. Pray as the Spirit leads you for others to "stand perfect and complete in all the will of God."

c. **Ephesians 1:15-16**
"Therefore I also, after I heard of your faith in the Lord Jesus and your love for all the saints, do not cease to give thanks for you, making mention of you in my prayers."

What should you not cease to do?

What does it mean to "make mention" of someone in prayer?

d. **Ephesians 6:18-19**
"Praying always with all prayer and supplication in the Spirit, being watchful to this end with all perseverance and supplication for all the saints. . . "

Whom should you pray for?

Who are the "saints"?

4. **Pray for pastors, teachers, and preachers.**
Spiritual leaders need prayer. Those called to lead, teach and preach face constant opposition from the enemy and he would love nothing more than to silence them and hurt those who follow their lead. That's why pastors, teachers and preachers need prayer for boldness, strength and open doors to steadily proclaim the gospel and teach the Word.

a. **2 Thessalonians 3:1**
"Finally, brethren, pray for us, that the Word of the Lord may run swiftly and be glorified, just as it is with you."

In what way should you pray for preachers and the Word to make an impact?

REVELATION DROP: Have you ever noticed what happens in Acts 13:44? The Word "ran swiftly," and, listen to this, *"On the next Sabbath almost the whole city came together to hear the Word of God."* What if you prayed for your city to have an Acts 13:44 experience with the Word of God?

b. **Colossians 4:2-4 NLT**
"Devote yourselves to prayer with an alert mind and a thankful heart. Pray for us, too, that God will give us many opportunities to speak about his mysterious plan concerning Christ. That is why I am here in chains. Pray that I will proclaim this message as clearly as I should."

How should you pray for spiritual leaders and preachers?

REVELATION DROP: If pastors and spiritual leaders did not need prayer, there would not be so many references to it in the New Testament; but the truth is apostles, prophets, evangelists, pastors and teachers do need prayer so they can properly lead those in their care. Every spiritual leader needs prayer for these four things: open doors to proclaim the gospel (Colossians 4:3,4); boldness and clarity to speak the Word (Ephesians 6:19); deliverance from adversaries and unbelieving enemies (1 Corinthians 16:9); and encouragement in times of trouble (2 Corinthians 1:11).

I love this quote from Stephen Nielsen's book *Prayer A to Z*. He quotes the legendary E.M. Bounds regarding the prayers needed for pastors and spiritual leaders: *"They need prayer more than others because they have more responsibilities, and they influence more people. If Satan overtakes a pastor, for example, the whole congregation is affected. Therefore, when we pray for a pastor, we are in effect praying for the whole church. I don't think there has ever been a great preacher or evangelist that did not have faithful prayer warriors interceding for them. Peter Wagner in his book Prayer Shield tells of two great evangelists, Charles Finney and Billy Graham, who each had their faithful intercessors praying for them. Finney had one known as 'Father Nash' who frequently traveled with him; and Billy Graham had Pearl Goode, which Graham himself has attributed much of his evangelism power to."*[2]

   c.   **Matthew 9:36-38**

"But when He saw the multitudes, He was moved with compassion for them, because they were weary and scattered, like sheep having no shepherd. Then He said to His disciples, 'The harvest truly is plentiful, but the laborers are few. Therefore pray the Lord of the harvest to send out laborers into His harvest.'"

Why is Jesus moved with compassion?

What does Jesus say is "plentiful" and "few"?

What does He tell us to pray for? Why?

5.   **Pray for the lost—2 Peter 3:9.**

"The Lord is not slack concerning His promise, as some count slackness, but is longsuffering toward us, not willing that any should perish but that all should come to repentance."

What is He waiting for?

Does God want anyone to perish?

Who does God want to come to repentance?

REVELATION DROP: The Bible tells us that Jesus is coming again, and in the last days, scoffers will ask, "Where is the promise of His coming?" The Lord is not slack about His promise to return, but according to this passage, the reason He hasn't returned is because He is patiently waiting for those who are lost and will repent—to come to Christ.

We can pray for the lost with authority and faith based upon God's revealed will. Let me share what God did in our family with the hopes that you are encouraged to pray for your family in the same way.

As the first born-again believer in my family, my top prayer was for the salvation of my entire "blood, step, and in-law" relatives. This is how the Lord led me to pray.

I knew that according to 1 Timothy 2:4, God's will and desire is for all people to be saved. According to 2 Peter 3:9, it is not His will that anyone perish, but that all repent and come to Jesus. I saw in Romans 2:4 that it is His kindness that leads people to repentance. And finally, I knew that according to Romans 10:13-15, in order to call on the Lord to be saved, they had to hear the Gospel. So, I prayed according to these truths in God's Word (His will) and since I knew I was praying according to His will, I knew He heard me; and since I knew He heard me, then I knew I had the petition I had desired—the salvation of my family!

I prayed specifically that God would reveal Himself to them through gospel preachers (me or others). I prayed they would think about eternity, experience His kindness—and be moved to repent of their sins. I knew God was going to work in ways I couldn't always see—revealing Himself to them and bringing the gospel to them so they could turn to Jesus, believe and be saved. I knew He would give me boldness and the open doors I needed to share the gospel with my family members—and, He did! Within a two-year time period, ten people in my immediate family (mom/stepdad, dad/stepmom, three sisters, and brothers-in-law) received Jesus as their Lord.

6. **Pray for those in your heart—Philippians 1:3-11.**

"I thank my God upon every remembrance of you, always in every prayer of mine making request for you all with joy, for your fellowship in the gospel from the first day until now, being confident of this very thing, that He who has begun a good work in you will complete it until the day of Jesus Christ; just as it is right for me to think this of you all, because I have you in my heart, inasmuch as both in my chains and in the defense and confirmation of the gospel, you all are partakers with me of grace. For God is my witness, how greatly I long for you all with the affection of Jesus Christ. And this I pray, that your love may abound still more and more in knowledge and all discernment, that you may approve the things that are excellent, that you may be sincere and without offense till the day of Christ, being filled with the fruits of righteousness which are by Jesus Christ, to the glory and praise of God."

Circle the word "prayer" or "pray" in this passage.

In the first part, what does the Apostle Paul say about his prayers for these believers?

In the last part, what does Paul pray for them?

When we identify those God has put in our heart, it's easy to pray for them. Who is in your heart?

REVELATION DROP: Who has the Lord put in your heart? Pray for them and watch what God will do. When I think about the people God has put in our hearts over the years, I am reminded of what a joy it is to pray for them. When the Lord puts people in your heart, it's easy to pray because He also puts His love for them in your heart, too. My husband and I, and our ministry, have been the beneficiaries of these kinds of prayers. I can think of several people who consistently pray for my husband and I, simply because the Lord has put us in their hearts. They don't sound the trumpet when they pray; they just pray. Words cannot express our gratitude—we know their prayers help us fulfill our God-given assignment. Heaven keeps good records and I know they will be rewarded for all that they have done in prayer. Who has the Lord put in your heart? Your prayers will help them to "*. . . grow and mature, standing complete and perfect in the beauty of God's plan . . .*" (Colossians 4:13 TPT).

7. **Pray for persecuted Christians.**

   a.   **2 Corinthians 1:8-11 NLT**
   "We think you ought to know, dear brothers and sisters, about the trouble we went through in the province of Asia. We were crushed and overwhelmed beyond our ability to endure, and we thought we would never live through it. In fact, we expected to die. But as a result, we stopped relying on ourselves and learned to rely only on God, who raises the dead. And he did rescue us from mortal danger, and he will rescue us again. We have placed our confidence in him, and he will continue to rescue us. And you are helping us by praying for us. Then many people will give thanks because God has graciously answered so many prayers for our safety."

   How does the Apostle Paul describe the difficulties and persecutions he faced?

   What role does the prayers of the believers play in their safety?

   What would have happened had they not prayed?

   REVELATION DROP: Have you prayed for persecuted Christians lately? We have brothers and sisters around the world who are paying a mighty high price for the faith that many of us freely enjoy. Many of us have never experienced persecution, much less persecution to the point of martyrdom. We can help them by praying for them. Whether it's a young believer being bullied at school for their faith, a pastor being shamed and canceled on social media for their Biblical messages or men and women in other lands who are being held captive because of their faith in Jesus. Take a moment right now to pray for their faith, boldness, safety, comfort and deliverance.

    b.   **Philippians 1:19 NLT**

"For I know that as you pray for me and the Spirit of Jesus Christ helps me, this will lead to my deliverance."

What role does prayer play in helping to deliver those being persecuted for their faith?

8.   **Pray for your enemies—Matthew 5:43-44.**

"You have heard that it was said, 'You shall love your neighbor and hate your enemy.' But I say to you, love your enemies, bless those who curse you, do good to those who hate you, and pray for those who spitefully use you and persecute you."

What should you do to your enemies, haters, and persecutors?

C.   PRAY WITH OTHERS

I love to pray alone with God. This is where intimacy with God is developed, but there is something about praying together with others—whether with one other person, in a small group, or in a large prayer setting—it seems there is additional power and advancements that can be made. Praying with others in a small-group setting has blessed my prayer life in profound ways.

When I think about the prayer groups I have been a part of, I cannot overstate their importance. When I was in college, I was in several prayer groups where we sought the Lord and then went out to local bars, beaches or the streets to share the gospel. While I was in Bible School, I attended prayer school and not only was I taught about prayer, but more importantly, I caught the "spirit of prayer." When our kids were little, I was in a Moms in Touch prayer group with several other mothers, and together we prayed for our kids on a regular basis. In our church, we have offered a variety of opportunities for small and large groups to meet together to pray. I can't imagine my life or ministry without having had those experiences to pray with others. I encourage you to look for opportunities in your church or small group to pray with other believers.

1.   **Acts 1:13-15**

"And when they had entered, they went up into the upper room where they were staying: Peter, James, John, and Andrew; Philip and Thomas; Bartholomew and Matthew; James the son of Alphaeus and Simon the Zealot; and Judas the son of James. These all continued with one accord in prayer and supplication, with the women and Mary the mother of Jesus, and with His brothers. And in those days Peter stood up in the midst of the disciples (altogether the number of names was about a hundred and twenty)."

The early church started with a large prayer meeting!

How many people are gathered to pray?

2.   **Acts 4:24-31**

"So when they heard that, they raised their voice to God with one accord and said: 'Lord, You are God, who made heaven and earth and the sea, and all that is in them, who by the mouth of

Your servant David have said:' 'Why did the nations rage, and the people plot vain things? The kings of the earth took their stand, and the rulers were gathered together against the LORD and against His Christ.' For truly against Your holy Servant Jesus, whom You anointed, both Herod and Pontius Pilate, with the Gentiles and the people of Israel, were gathered together to do whatever Your hand and Your purpose determined before to be done. Now, Lord, look on their threats, and grant to Your servants that with all boldness they may speak Your word, by stretching out Your hand to heal, and that signs and wonders may be done through the name of Your holy Servant Jesus.' And when they had prayed, the place where they were assembled together was shaken; and they were all filled with the Holy Spirit, and they spoke the word of God with boldness."

How do the disciples begin their prayers?

What do they ask for?

How does God answer?

REVELATION DROP: Notice the "formula" for prayer. They magnify and praise God. Then they remind God and themselves of His promises and previous works of greatness. They recognize God's present-tense willingness to help them, and they make their specific request known to the Lord. And what does God do? He answers!

3.   **Matthew 18:19-20**

"Again I say to you that if two of you agree on earth concerning anything that they ask, it will be done for them by My Father in heaven. For where two or three are gathered together in My name, I am there in the midst of them."

When two or more people are gathered together, how should they pray?

What will our Father do?

D.   PRAY IT OUT

What verse or passages stood out to you in this chapter? What truths stirred your heart?

Take a moment to pray and put these things into practice.

1.   Blue Letter Bible, s.v. "lambanō," April 16, 2021, https://www.blueletterbible.org//lang/lexicon/lexicon.cfm?Strongs=G2983&t=KJV.
2.   E. M. Bounds, Prayer and Praying Men, (Grand Rapids: Baker Book House, 1977), 103.

SECTION 4:

THE "WHY" OF PRAYER

CHAPTER 9:

THE "WHY" OF PRAYER - PART 1

"Heaven is full of answers for which nobody ever bothered to ask."
Billy Graham

Why pray? Do our prayers really make any difference? (Yes!) Isn't God going to do what He wants to do anyway? (No!) Do our prayers influence or persuade God, or do they influence and persuade us? (All of the above!)

The "why" of prayer can be answered in many ways.

>> One reason to pray is to draw near and enjoy fellowship with the Lord.
>> Another reason to pray is to ask God for the things we and others need.
>> Another reason to pray is bring forth lasting fruit.

Let's look at several more reasons we should pray.

A. JESUS WANTS TO WORK WITH US

When we pray, we are working together with God to request, say, declare and prophesy over our future. Our friend, Rev. Mary Frances Varallo once said it this way, *"Through prayer, we create the track we run on."* This is true—we can "pray ahead." By praying out the track of our lives, we get ahead of the curve and in doing so, the Lord makes the crooked place straight for us. He gives us the wisdom we need. He opens the proper doors and closes distractions. Prayer helps to "grease the skids" for our lives.

Some people assume that because God is the Almighty, and all of creation is His "ball and bat," He can do anything He wants whenever He wants! However, in His sovereignty, He doesn't do what He wants. (If so, He would make everyone get saved.) Instead, what He did do was send His only begotten Son to this earth to die on a cross so that whoever believes in Him would have everlasting life (John 3:16). He gives us the choice to believe, receive and respond to Him.

God doesn't arbitrarily do anything He wants to do because He has limited Himself to His Word. He created this world to operate on the spiritual principles of faith. He won't violate His own word or say, "I was just kidding." He won't grow impatient with an I'll-just-do-it-Myself attitude. No, He will always be true to His own character. If, with His Word, He has promised His blessings to us, and if He has established a way for us to experience those blessings, He has obligated Himself to operate *that* way. He won't play the "I am Sovereign" card to override Himself.

That's where our prayers come in. He desires to partner with man to fulfill His will on the earth. We are joint-heirs and co-creators with Him as we travel through our time on earth (Romans 8:17, John 14:12-

14, 1 Corinthians 3:9). It is as the well-known preacher and hymn-writer John Wesley said, *"God does nothing except in response to believing prayer."*[1] When we learn what He has promised and what He has purposed, and when we make that our prayers; we are working with Him; and then He is able to do what He desires to do in the earth.

1. **2 Corinthians 6:1**

   "We then, as workers together with Him also plead with you not to receive the grace of God in vain."

   Who works with God?

2. **1 Corinthians 3:9**

   "For we are God's fellow workers; you are God's field, you are God's building."

   Who is a fellow worker with God?

REVELATION DROP: We can see throughout Scripture; God works with us. When it comes to prayer, the Lord doesn't pray for us, but He helps us pray. Romans tell us, *"Likewise the Spirit also helps in our weaknesses. For we do not know what we should pray for as we ought, but the Spirit Himself makes intercession for us with groanings which cannot be uttered. Now He who searches the hearts knows what the mind of the Spirit is, because He makes intercession for the saints according to the will of God"* (8:26-27).

As mentioned, God is Sovereign in His eternal purposes and providential wisdom, but He doesn't do everything arbitrarily or apart from us; and we can't do anything apart from Him. The Lord wants and needs us to pray as His delegates on earth. This started in the Garden of Eden. God desired a relationship with Adam and Eve, and they were to co-rule the earth with God's authority (Genesis 1:26-31). This has been God's desire throughout the Bible—He desires to empower mankind to work with Him.

Through Jesus death, burial and resurrection, we have been saved and repositioned in life! We have been redeemed, raised up and seated with Christ in heavenly places (Eph 2:6). We are workers with God! Prayer is one of the major ways we can partner with God.

Kenneth E. Hagin described it this way, *"The trouble with us is that we've preached a 'cross' religion, and we need to preach a 'throne' religion. By that I mean that people have thought they were supposed to remain at the cross. Some have received the baptism in the Holy Spirit, have backed up to the cross, and have stayed there ever since. The cross is actually a place of defeat, whereas the Resurrection is a place of triumph. When you preach the cross, you're preaching death, and you leave people in death."*[2]

This is an essential truth when it comes to praying effectively. We don't pray from a defeated position, rather we pray from the place of victory seated with Christ at the Father's right hand! We don't pray as those *standing on earth looking up*, we pray as those who are *seated in heaven looking down*. From that position, we don't pray "for victory" we pray "from victory." Can you see that? Let's talk about how to pray this way—in faith (not doubt), from victory (not defeat) and with joy (not depression.) Praying this way will revolutionize your prayer life.

B. JESUS TOLD US TO ASK

Apparently, in God's kingdom, some things won't just happen unless we *ask*. It turns out, unless we pray and ask God for particular things, we will not receive them. Remember, God wants to work *with* us. Our part is to ask, and God's part is to answer. Let's see this spelled out in God's Word.

We will revisit many of the Scriptures we have already looked at, but let's look at them again in light of the Lord's command to *ask*.

Take a moment to circle the word *ask* in each passage in this section.

1.   **Matthew 7:7-11**
        "Ask, and it will be given to you; seek, and you will find; knock, and it will be opened to you. For everyone who asks receives, and he who seeks finds, and to him who knocks it will be opened. Or what man is there among you who, if his son asks for bread, will give him a stone? Or if he asks for a fish, will he give him a serpent? If you then, being evil, know how to give good gifts to your children, how much more will your Father who is in heaven give good things to those who ask Him!"

        What three things are we told to do when it comes to prayer?

        What will happen for everyone who asks?

        What will happen for everyone who seeks?

        What will happen for everyone who knocks?

        What will your heavenly Father do for *you* when you ask Him?

        REVELATION DROP: Again, let's look at the word *ask*. According to *Strong's Greek Lexicon*, it's biblical meanings include, "ask, beg, call for, crave, desire, require." [3] According to *Vine's Expository Dictionary,* to ask "suggests the attitude of a suppliant, the petition of one who is lesser in position than he to whom the petition is made; e.g., in the case of men in asking something from God; a child from a parent; a subject from a king."[4]

        For us, we (the lesser) *ask, beg, call for, crave, desire,* and *require* God (the Greater) to fulfill His Word, His promise, or His purpose. Asking is our way of accessing what belongs to us in Christ. Interestingly, God knows what we have need of, but He waits for us to ask Him for those things before He does them for us.

2. **John 15:7**
    "If you abide in Me, and My words abide in you, you will ask what you desire, and it shall be done for you."

    Who are you to abide in?

    What is to abide in you?

    What can you ask God for?

    What will be His response?

    REVELATION DROP: To abide is to stay in Christ and His love. It's no wonder Jesus could make such a generous promise, He knows that when we abide in Him and His Word abides in us, our desires will be aligned with His.

3. **John 14:13-14**
    "And whatever you ask in My name, that I will do, that the Father may be glorified in the Son. If you ask anything in My name, I will do it."

    What can you ask the Father for in Jesus' name?

    What will He do?

    Who gets the glory?

    God always gets the glory; we get the benefit!

4. **John 16:23-24**
    "And in that day you will ask Me nothing. Most assuredly, I say to you, whatever you ask the Father in My name He will give you. Until now you have asked nothing in My name. Ask, and you will receive, that your joy may be full."

    What day is Jesus talking about?

    What can you ask the Father for?

    In order to receive, what do you have to do?

What result will you experience when you receive your requests?

5. **1 John 5:14-15**

"Now this is the confidence that we have in Him, that if we ask anything according to His will, He hears us. And if we know that He hears us, whatever we ask, we know that we have the petitions that we have asked of Him."

Can you have confidence in God and His ability to hear your prayers and answer them?

What do you know is true if you ask anything according to His will?

If you know God hears you when you ask, then what else do you know?

How do you know what God's will is?

6. **James 1:5-8**

"If any of you lacks wisdom, let him ask of God, who gives to all liberally and without reproach, and it will be given to him. But let him ask in faith, with no doubting, for he who doubts is like a wave of the sea driven and tossed by the wind. For let not that man suppose that he will receive anything from the Lord; he is a double-minded man, unstable in all his ways."

If you lack or need wisdom, what should you do?

What will God do?

How should you ask?

If you ask in doubt, what can you expect?

7. **James 4:2-3**

"Yet you do not have because you do not ask. You ask and do not receive, because you ask amiss, that you may spend it on your pleasures."

Why do you not have the things you need or desire?

Why do you not receive the things you ask for?

REVELATION DROP: Clearly, our *asking* makes a difference! We've been given the authority, responsibility and privilege to pray and ask God for the things we and others need!

C. JESUS GAVE US "THE LORD'S PRAYER" AS A MODEL

Another big "why" when it comes to prayer is related to the responsibility God has given us to pray for His will to be done on earth, as it is in heaven. Jesus gave us the pattern for praying this way in The Lord's Prayer.

1.   **Luke 11:1-5**
      "Now it came to pass, as He was praying in a certain place, when He ceased, that one of His disciples said to Him, "Lord, teach us to pray, as John also taught his disciples." So He said to them, "When you pray, say:

      Our Father in heaven, hallowed be Your name. Your kingdom come. Your will be done on earth as it is in heaven. Give us day by day our daily bread. And forgive us our sins, for we also forgive everyone who is indebted to us. And do not lead us into temptation, but deliver us from the evil one."

      What do the disciples ask Jesus to teach them?

      What does Jesus teach them?

2.   **Matthew 6:9-13**
      "In this manner, therefore, pray: Our Father in heaven, hallowed be Your name. Your kingdom come. Your will be done on earth as it is in heaven. Give us this day our daily bread. And forgive us our debts, as we forgive our debtors. And do not lead us into temptation, but deliver us from the evil one. For Yours is the kingdom and the power and the glory forever. Amen."

      In this passage, there are six prayer pitstops embedded within Jesus' words, can you identify them?

      REVELATION DROP: I have heard The Lord's Prayer sung in the most beautiful ways. In fact, I grew up calling it the Our Father and we often recited this pray and sang it verbatim. Did you? However, it turns out, Jesus didn't necessarily teach The Lord's Prayer as a rote prayer to memorize, but rather Jesus calls it a "manner" (or model) for prayer (Matthew 6:9). Bible Commentator, Chuck Smith describes Jesus' words this way, *"He is clearly giving to the disciples a model or form for prayer. It is not something to be repeated by rote in vain repetition, for He has just warned against vain repetitions in prayer. He has given to them a model."*[5]

      In this prayer model, we see an outline, a pattern, or a "table of contents" with six prayer pitstops that we can follow in prayer. When I first heard someone teach The Lord's Prayer in this way, it really resonated and helped me to stay focused in my own prayer life. As a result, I've been using this model for many years. I like it because it gives structure to my prayers, while at the same time allowing me to flow with the Holy Spirit's leading at each pitstop. My husband and I have used this pattern in prayer to take a prayer drive around our city, and as we have driven north, east, south, and west; we've prayed each of these pitstops for our church and region. Here is a general idea of some of the ways I pray at each pitstop:

a. **Pitstop #1: Our Father in heaven, hallowed be Your name.**

At this pitstop, I like to enter God's presence to thank, praise, and magnify His Name! Specifically, I pray from my heart to worship God as my Father, to exalt Jesus as Lord and to thank the Holy Spirit as my Helper. *Pitstop #1 helps us to look up to our heavenly Father.*

b. **Pitstop #2: Your will be done on earth as it is in heaven.**

At this pitstop, I like to pray for God's will to be done on earth as it is in heaven—in my sphere of influence. This is where I pray God's Word for my for my husband, our kids, and every blood, step-, and in-law member of my family. This is also when I endeavor to be led by the Spirit to pray and declare God's word and His will to be done in the lives of my friends, our ministry and social media partners and followers, our church family, our country, and God's purposes for His church and those in nations around the world. *Pitstop #2 helps us to pray for God's will to be done.*

c. **Pitstop #3: Give us day-by-day our daily bread.**

At this pitstop, I like to pray and thank God for the bread I need each day. The Bible describes *bread* as God's Word, His healing power, and more; so, I ask the Lord for these things. Jesus calls Himself the "bread of life," so when I pray for my daily bread, I pray for more of Jesus to be revealed in and through my life. *Pitstop #3 helps us to pray for our daily needs.*

d. **Pitstop #4: And forgive us our debts as we forgive our debtors.**

At this pitstop, I like to check my heart to be certain I am not holding anything against anyone. If any hurt feelings or sense of offense have crept in, I take time to release those individuals to the Lord, and I choose to forgive them. Meanwhile, I thank the Lord He forgives me for any hurt or offense I have caused Him or others. *Pitstop #4 helps us keep our hearts free from offense.*

e. **Pitstop #5: And do not lead us into temptation, but deliver us from the evil one.**

At this pitstop, I like to thank the Lord for the victory and authority Jesus has purchased for us. I declare the name of Jesus, the blood of Jesus, the angels of God and the power of His Word over my life, my family, and our church and others as the Spirit leads. At this pitstop, I take time to put on my spiritual armor to resist temptation and to enforce the devil's defeat and Jesus' victory in our lives. *Pitstop #5 helps us pray from victory.*

f. **Pitstop #6: For Yours is the kingdom and the power and the glory forever.**

At this pitstop, I like to wrap up my prayer time by praising the Lord and acknowledging that all the kingdoms, power, and glory are His. This is a good pitstop to thank the Lord for His goodness and the benefits of such a wonderful life with Him. *Pitstop #6 helps us to give God all the glory.*

I hope this encouraged you! When we pray using The Lord's Prayer, we can easily spend one hour or more in prayer—with plenty to talk about! Can you see how rich The Lord's Prayer is as a model and pattern for prayer? I believe you will enjoy incorporating this prayer outline into your own prayer life. There are so many different directions you could pray at each pitstop. The important thing is to be led by the Spirit and follow your heart—then watch His kingdom come and His will be done on earth as it is in heaven!

D.   PRAY IT OUT

What verse or passages stood out to you in this chapter? What truths stirred your heart?

Take a moment to pray and put these things into practice.

1. "John Wesley Quotes," Brainy Quote, June 10, 2021, https://www.brainyquote.com/quotes/john_wesley_524892.

2 "Top Quotes by Kenneth E. Hagin," Quote Master, June 1, 2021, https://www.quotemaster.org/q00f5ea0ef545eb370cf3406891298c20.

3. Blue Letter Bible, s.v. "aiteō," March 27, 2021. https://www.blueletterbible.org//lang/lexicon/lexicon.cfm?Strongs=G154&t=KJV.

4. Blue Letter Bible, s.v. "ask," June 1, 2021, https://www.blueletterbible.org/search/dictionary/viewtopic.cfm?topic=VT0000165.

5. Chuck Smith, "Sermon Notes for Matthew 6:9 by Chuck Smith," Blue Letter Bible. May 1, 2005, https://www.blueletterbible.org/Comm/smith_chuck/SermonNotes_Mat/Mat_99.cfm.

CHAPTER 10:

THE "WHY" OF PRAYER - PART 2

"Prayer is not an exercise, it is the life."
Oswald Chambers

Let's talk about another "why"—the "why" of praying to bring forth fruit.

In the same way that the rain brings forth fruit in the natural world (whether we're talking about bananas, apples, or watermelon) so, too, our prayers bring forth fruit in God's kingdom—the fruit of souls saved, lives changed, and believers empowered.

A. GOD NEEDS OUR PRAYERS TO BRING FORTH FRUIT

One of the best Bible-based metaphors I've heard on the power of prayer to bring forth fruit has to do with the natural rain cycle. God often uses His creation to teach us rich spiritual truths. Romans tells us that God reveals Himself through creation itself, *"For ever since the creation of the world His invisible nature and attributes, that is, His eternal power and divinity, have been made intelligible and clearly discernible in and through the things that have been made (His handiworks)" (Romans 1:20 AMPC).* Let's study the relationship between God's creation of the rain cycle as it relates to prayer and fruit.

1. **God wants us to produce fruit—John 15:16.**
   "You did not choose Me, but I chose you and appointed you that you should go and bear fruit, and that your fruit should remain, that whatever you ask the Father in My name He may give you."

   Who chose you?

   What does Jesus want you to do?

   What does He want the fruit to do?

   What does He say you can ask the Father to do?

   REVELATION DROP: Jesus chose us to bring forth lasting fruit, and then He promised that whatever we ask of the Father (including our request for fruit!) He will give it to us. The fruit

God wants to produce through us is the fruit of the Spirit (love, joy, peace, patience, kindness, goodness, faithfulness, gentleness and self-control) and the fruit of people coming to Christ (people being saved and becoming His disciples). In prayer, we can work with the Lord to produce fruit.

2.   **God is waiting for fruit—James 5:7-8.**
"Therefore be patient, brethren, until the coming of the Lord. See how the farmer waits for the precious fruit of the earth, waiting patiently for it until it receives the early and latter rain. You also be patient. Establish your hearts, for the coming of the Lord is at hand."

Jesus is coming again, but He, like the farmer, is waiting; what is He waiting for?

So, if Jesus is waiting for the fruit of the earth, and if the fruit of the earth is waiting for rain, what should you pray for?

REVELATION DROP: Why hasn't Jesus returned as He promised He would? He is waiting for the fruit of the earth—the harvest of souls, precious souls from every tribe, tongue, and nation. He does not want anyone to perish; He wants everyone to repent and come to Him. This is the precious fruit of the earth. This fruit cannot come into fruition until it receives the rain. That's where prayer comes in. We need to pray for rain.

Remember what Peter wrote? There have always been scoffers questioning the Lord, His Word, and His return. Look at this: *"Scoffers will come in the last days, walking according to their own lusts, and saying, "Where is the promise of His coming? For since the fathers fell asleep, all things continue as they were from the beginning of creation. . . . But, beloved, do not forget this one thing, that with the Lord one day is as a thousand years, and a thousand years as one day. The Lord is not slack concerning His promise, as some count slackness, but is longsuffering toward us, not willing that any should perish but that all should come to repentance"* (2 Peter 3:3,4,8,9).

In His mercy, the Lord has been patient, but you can be sure Jesus is coming again! He is waiting for the precious fruit of the earth and giving all those who will repent an opportunity to hear the Gospel to do so.

3.   **God wants us to pray for rain, just like Elijah—James 5:17-18.**
"Elijah was a man with a nature like ours, and he prayed earnestly that it would not rain; and it did not rain on the land for three years and six months. And he prayed again, and the heaven gave rain, and the earth produced its fruit."

You can see that Elijah was a man just like us. He was not special; he had a human nature like any of us. Elijah saw miraculous results from his prayers for rain.

What did Elijah pray for earnestly?

What was the result of his first prayer?

When Elijah prayed again, what did he pray for?

What was the result of his second prayer?

What was the result of the rain?

REVELATION DROP: Let me share a few insights on how Elijah prayed for rain and how we should too. Elijah didn't just arbitrarily decide, of his own volition, to pray for the rain to start and stop. Each time Elijah prayed, he prayed according to the will of the Lord. He heard from God, and according to the "word of the Lord" he had received, he prayed. (1 Kings 17:1-7, 18:1-2, 45) We can do the very same thing. When we hear from God through His Word or through the voice of His Spirit, we follow that prompting, and we pray accordingly. Our prayers start with God. He gives us His Word, and He prompts our spirit to pray His will to be done on earth as it is in heaven.

B. GOD REVEALS HIS PRAYER PLAN IN THE RAIN CYCLE

Before He comes again, Jesus is waiting for all the precious fruit of the earth—the souls of those who will come to Christ. In order for the fruit to come forth, it needs rain. When we follow God's instructions to "pray for rain," what exactly are we praying for? God has revealed it to us through the natural rain cycle. Let's look at both the natural and spiritual truths in rain.

THE RAIN CYCLE: NATURAL AND SPIRITUAL

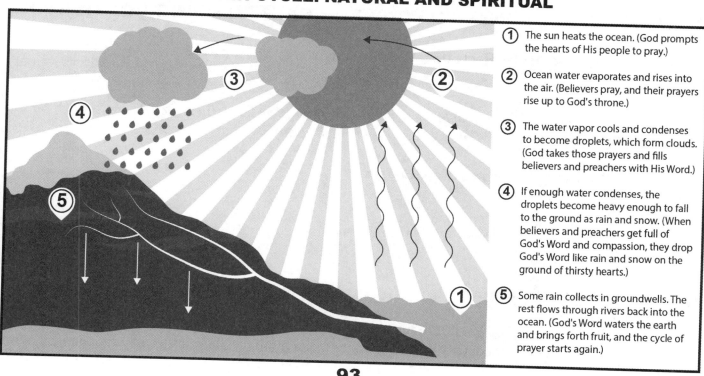

① The sun heats the ocean. (God prompts the hearts of His people to pray.)

② Ocean water evaporates and rises into the air. (Believers pray, and their prayers rise up to God's throne.)

③ The water vapor cools and condenses to become droplets, which form clouds. (God takes those prayers and fills believers and preachers with His Word.)

④ If enough water condenses, the droplets become heavy enough to fall to the ground as rain and snow. (When believers and preachers get full of God's Word and compassion, they drop God's Word like rain and snow on the ground of thirsty hearts.)

⑤ Some rain collects in groundwells. The rest flows through rivers back into the ocean. (God's Word waters the earth and brings forth fruit, and the cycle of prayer starts again.)

Let's look at each of these phases and the way the rain cycle works.

1. **Step One: Water Heats Up**
   -In the natural, the sun *heats* the ocean, lakes, rivers, and other sources of water.
   -Spiritually, God *"heats up"* the hearts of believers and prompts them to pray.

2. **Step Two: Water Evaporates**
   -Naturally, the water *evaporates and rises* into the air.
   -Spiritually, believers pray, and their *prayers "rise up"* to His throne.

3. **Step Three: Clouds Form**
   -In the natural, the water vapor cools and condenses to become droplets, which form *clouds*.
   -Spiritually, as believers pray, God forms their "evaporated prayers" into *"clouds"* (believers and preachers) filled with His Word.

4. **Step Four: Rain Comes Down**
   -Naturally, if enough water condenses, the *drops* become heavy and *fall to the ground as rain*.
   -Spiritually, when believers and preachers get full of God's Word and compassion, they *drop God's Word like rain* and snow on the ground of thirsty hearts.

5. **Step Five: Fruit Comes Forth**
   -In the natural, rain waters the earth and *brings forth fruit*, some rain collects in ground wells, and the rest flows through rivers back into the oceans.
   -Spiritually, God's Word waters the earth and *brings forth fruit*, and the prayer rain cycle starts all over again.

What an amazing process! The best part is that God wants us to participate in it through prayer. Let's see this amazing step-by-step "pray for rain" plan throughout God's Word.

C. GOD TOLD US HOW TO PRAY FOR RAIN TO BRING FORTH FRUIT

1. **Step One: Water Heats Up—God Prompts You to Ask for Rain**

   Zechariah 10:1
   "Ask the Lord for rain in the time of the latter rain. The Lord will make flashing clouds; He will give them showers of rain, grass in the field for everyone."

   What are you supposed to ask God for?

   When are you supposed to ask Him for rain?

   What will the Lord do?

   REVELATION DROP: Through the prophet Zechariah, God told us to ask Him for rain. The good news is that not only does God ask us to pray for rain, He helps us pray for rain by moving upon our hearts to pray. I once heard a preacher describe prayer as a conversation that originates with God, and as He moves upon our hearts, our prayers are our response back to God. Prayer is His idea! He is the one who prompts our hearts to pray for rain. When we pray for rain, we are praying His will back to Him. He wants (and needs) us to pray for rain.

2. **Step Two: Water Evaporates—You Ask the Lord for Rain**

   Psalm 135:5-7
   "For I know that the Lord is great, and our Lord is above all gods. Whatever the Lord pleases He does, in heaven and in earth, in the seas and in all deep places. He causes the vapors to ascend from the ends of the earth; He makes lightning for the rain; He brings the wind out of His treasuries."

   What does the Lord cause to ascend?

   REVELATION DROP: In the natural world of the rain cycle, ocean water evaporates and forms clouds. In the spiritual world of the rain cycle, our prayers are like vapors (evaporation), which rise to the Lord, and He uses them to fill clouds too. You may be wondering how this works. Let's continue.

3. **Step Three: Clouds Form—Your Prayers Fill Clouds with Rain**

   Ecclesiastes 11:3
   "If the clouds are full of rain, they empty themselves upon the earth; And if a tree falls to the south or the north, in the place where the tree falls, there it shall lie."

   When clouds are full of rain, what do they do?

   REVELATION DROP: As we pray, just as in the natural evaporation process, vapors fill clouds, so, too, God uses our "prayer vapors" to fill clouds with rain, not literal clouds in the sky, instead the clouds God fills are people.

   In the Bible, clouds are a metaphor for people (Hebrews 12:1). When we pray, our prayers ascend like vapors to God's throne, and then He fill clouds (people, believers, preachers—His Church) with "rain." When the clouds (people) are full they "rain" and empty themselves out on the earth!

   This begs the question—*what is rain?* If our prayers ascend to God's throne and He fills clouds (His Church) with the rain needed to produce the precious fruit of the earth, what exactly is the rain?

4. **Step Four: Rain Comes Down—Rain is God's Presence and the Teaching of God's Word**

   When we pray for the rain or when we sing songs and ask for the Lord to "rain down," we are not asking for pixie dust or a series of holy goosebumps, instead the rain we are asking for two things: *His presence* and *His Word*. Let's look at this.

a. **God's presence is like the rain—Hosea 6:3**
"Let us know, let us pursue the knowledge of the Lord. His going forth is established as the morning. He will come to us like the rain, like the latter and former rain to the earth."

Who comes to you as the rain?

REVELATION DROP: The presence of the Lord is like rain. Have you experienced His sweet presence in your life? This is rain! The rain of His presence produces fruit in our lives—the fruit of the Spirit, the fruit of being a bold witness for Christ, and much more fruit that remains. Not only is His presence like sweet rain now, one day the Lord Jesus will come to us in His second coming as the rain.

When we pray for rain, we are praying for the presence of Jesus to flow into and out of His Church (that is into and out of believers—we are His clouds) to cover all the earth. A church full of believers, who are also full of the presence of Jesus, is the perfect "big cloud" God can use to pour out the rain of His presence upon those who come into contact with it.

But that's not all; the rain is also a reference to God's Word. Let's look at this.

b. **God's Word is like the rain—Deuteronomy 32:1-3 NLT**
"Listen, O heavens, and I will speak! Hear, O earth, the words that I say! Let My teaching fall on you like rain; let My speech settle like dew, let My words fall like rain on tender grass, like gentle showers on young plants. I will proclaim the name of the LORD; how glorious is our God!"

What falls on the earth like rain?

What settles like dew?

What falls like rain on tender grass and showers on young plants?

REVELATION DROP: The teaching and proclamation of God's Word is rain. When we pray for rain, we are praying for the Lord to "rain down" His words upon hungry hearts. When we pray for rain, we are praying for the Word of God to pour out from His Church upon people all over the earth!

Can you see what the rain represents and why the Lord told us to ask for it? When we pray for rain, we are asking for these two things:

>> The rain as the manifested presence of the Lord
>> The rain as the teaching of God's Word

Now, the big question is, what does the rain do? This is where the fruit comes forth.

c. **God's Word is like rain and produces fruit—Isaiah 55:9-11 NLT**

"For just as the heavens are higher than the earth, so My ways are higher than your ways and My thoughts higher than your thoughts. 'The rain and snow come down from the heavens and stay on the ground to water the earth. They cause the grain to grow, producing seed for the farmer and bread for the hungry. It is the same with My word. I send it out, and it always produces fruit. It will accomplish all I want it to, and it will prosper everywhere I send it.'"

What comes down from heaven?

What does rain do to the earth?

What does God's Word always produce and accomplish?

Where does God's Word prosper?

REVELATION DROP: God's Word is just like rain, and it always waters the earth and produces the fruit God intends. When we pray, God sends His Word by raising up, equipping, and sending His people (His Church) to preach the Good News near and far and His Word produces the fruit He intended.

5. **Step Five: Fruit Comes Forth—Your Prayers Help to Bring Forth the Fruit of the Earth**

James 5:7-8,17-18 NLT

"Dear brothers and sisters, be patient as you wait for the Lord's return. Consider the farmers who patiently wait for the rains in the fall and in the spring. They eagerly look for the valuable harvest to ripen. You, too, must be patient. Take courage, for the coming of the Lord is near. . . . Elijah was as human as we are, and yet when he prayed earnestly that no rain would fall, none fell for three and a half years! Then, when he prayed again, the sky sent down rain and the earth began to yield its crops."

What do farmers wait for?

What do they eagerly look for?

What did Elijah do?

What did the rain produce?

D. GOD'S PRAYER PLAN IS GENIUS

Can you see how powerful and simple your prayers can be in God's rain cycle? Through your prayers, you can play a part in bringing forth the precious fruit of the earth. Let's recap:

>> Jesus is not slow about coming again, but He is waiting for the precious fruit of the earth.

>> The precious fruit of the earth are people.

>> In order for the precious fruit of the earth to come forth—that is, in order for people around the world to come to Christ and to grow in Him—there must be rain. Just as in the natural, the fruit cannot come forth without rain; so, too, the precious fruit of the earth cannot come forth without rain.

>> The rain that is needed is the rain of God's manifested presence and the rain of His Word.

>> If Jesus is waiting for the precious fruit of the earth and the precious fruit of the earth is waiting for rain, what can we do to facilitate rain? It's simple: we pray. God tells us to ask Him for rain.

>> When we pray and ask God for rain, He will fill clouds (His people, His preachers and His Church) with rain (His presence and His Word), and as we proclaim Jesus and His Word throughout the earth, the precious fruit will come forth.

Does this rain prayer cycle fire you up to pray? I hope so!

If you look around and notice a lack of fruit—the precious fruit of the earth (people coming to Christ and growing in Him)—you know what to do. Pray.

It may sound like this, *"Father, according to Your Word, I pray for rain. Lord, fill Your people and fill Your Church, and send the rain—the rain of Your presence and the rain of Your Word. Lord send the rain to China. Send the rain to the White House. Send the rain to Broadway. Send the rain to my city. Send the rain to my family. Lord send the rain! Father, fill the clouds—your people, preachers, Your church with rain and let them boldly pour out with Your Presence and Your Word. Lord, send the rain! In Jesus' name, amen."* Then, pray in the Spirit (in your prayer language) as He leads you.

Go ahead; ask the Lord for rain!

E. PRAY IT OUT

What verse or passages stood out to you in this chapter? What truths stirred your heart?

Take a moment to pray and put these things into practice.

SECTION 5:

THE "HOW" OF PRAYER

CHAPTER 11:

THE "HOW" OF PRAYER - PART 1

"Every great movement of God can be traced to a kneeling figure."
D.L. Moody

It's funny how often we pray prayers the way we want to pray them, rather than the way God has asked us to pray. Our Father is full of mercy, but He is also a God of His Word, and He abides by the protocols He has set in place.

Imagine a child who wants something from their parents but just lies in bed and cries and whines for it—will they receive it? What about a teenager who treats his or her parents with disrespect and unkind words but then wants money from them to buy a new pair of shoes? How will the parents handle that? How about the young-adult son or daughter who treats their parents with an ungrateful and entitled attitude but expects the family business to be handed over to them? How is that going to work?

Of course, God is much more gracious and merciful that human parents, but He does not reward unbelief. He does not appreciate disrespect and unwholesome, faithless words. He is not honored by a sense of entitlement; rather He resists the proud and gives grace to the humble (1 Peter 5:5). Just as human parents want to bless their children, how much more does God? Just as human parents appreciate children who show respect and have a grateful attitude, how much more does God? That's exactly what Jesus tells us, *"If you, imperfect as you are, know how to lovingly take care of your children and give them what's best, how much more ready is your heavenly Father to give wonderful gifts to those who ask Him?" (Matthew 7:11 TPT).*

Let's look at several important basic how-tos when it comes to praying effectively.

A.   PRAY TO THE FATHER

This is a small, but important detail. We are to direct our prayers to God the Father. We covered this in an earlier chapter, but let's go over it again because it's so easy to miss.

1.   **John 16:23-24**
"And in that day you will ask Me nothing. Most assuredly, I say to you, whatever you ask the Father in My name He will give you. Until now you have asked nothing in My name. Ask, and you will receive, that your joy may be full."

Ever since the resurrection of Jesus, to whom do you direct your prayers?

REVELATION DROP: As we have already studied, when it comes to our petitions, Jesus said we wouldn't ask Him anything, but we would ask the Father. We direct our prayer requests to the Father in Jesus' name.

2. **Luke 11:1-2**

"Now it came to pass, as He was praying in a certain place, when He ceased, that one of His disciples said to Him, 'Lord, teach us to pray, as John also taught his disciples.' So He said to them, 'When you pray, say: Our Father in heaven, hallowed be Your name.'"

What do the disciples ask Jesus to teach them?

Who does Jesus tell us to direct our prayers to when we pray?

B.   PRAY THE WORD OF GOD

In order to pray effective prayers, we must pray according to God's will, and God's will is revealed in His Word. Jesus tells us to pray, *"Your kingdom come. Your will be done on earth as it is in heaven" (Matthew 6:10)*, so when we pray God's Word, we are praying God's will. Let's learn more about praying the Word of God.

1. **Psalm 138:2**

"I will worship toward Your holy temple, and praise Your name for Your lovingkindness and Your truth; for You have magnified Your word above all Your name."

What has God magnified above His name?

REVELATION DROP: God highly esteems His Word, so we should too.

2. **John 15:7**

"If you abide in Me, and My words abide in you, you will ask what you desire, and it shall be done for you."

What is supposed to "abide" in you?

When God's Word abides in you, how does that help you pray for the things you desire?

REVELATION DROP: When you abide in Jesus and His Word abides in you, you can have great confidence in prayer. You can ask for anything you desire, and He will grant it. That almost sounds like heresy, doesn't it? When Jesus said you could ask for "anything you desire," didn't He mean anything *God* desires? No, the Lord loves to give *you* the desires of your heart when you have been abiding in Him and His Word because He knows that your desires will be in perfect alignment with His desires.

3. **Jeremiah 1:12 AMPC**

"Then said the Lord to me, You have seen well, for I am alert and active, watching over My word to perform it."

What is God alert to and actively watching?

What will He perform?

4. **1 John 5:14-15**

"Now this is the confidence that we have in Him, that if we ask anything according to His will, He hears us. And if we know that He hears us, whatever we ask, we know that we have the petitions that we have asked of Him."

If you ask for anything according to His will, what can you be certain of?

If you know He hears you, what else can you be certain of?

REVELATION DROP: You can pray according to God's will by personalizing God's Word and praying it back to Him. Our friends, Steve and Tami, have pastored for many years and they are both pray-ers. In talking about prayer, they described how they pray the Word. They simply take scriptures that resonate with their hearts and they pray (say) it back to God. For example, 3 John 1:4 describes God's will for their children (natural and spiritual), *"I have no greater joy than to hear that my children walk in truth."* So, they personalize that passage in prayer and it sounds like this, *"Thank You, Father, we have no greater joy than to hear that our children (they mention them by name) walk in the truth of Your Word. Open up their hearts today to know, live, and walk in Your Word. In Jesus' name, amen."*

Easy, right? You can pray according to His will by praying His Word!

There are many great resources on praying God's Word. If you'd like a great resource loaded with Scriptural prayers, one of the first and best books I've read on this topic of praying God's Word is the classic, *Prayers That Avail Much* by Germaine Copeland. I read highly recommend it.

C.   PRAY IN THE NAME OF JESUS

Jesus has authorized us to use His name. We can *pray* and *say,* "in the name of Jesus," and when we do, all of heaven hears. His name is the name above all names in the universe. His name is the master key that opens every door. What a privilege to be authorized with the power of His name.

1. **Pray in Jesus' Name**

   a. **John 16:23**

   "And in that day you will ask Me nothing. Most assuredly, I say to you, whatever you ask the Father in My name He will give you. Until now you have asked nothing in My name. Ask, and you will receive, that your joy may be full."

   In whose name do you pray and ask the Father?

   What will He do?

   What will be the result of answered requests?

   b. **Acts 4:24, 29-31**

   "'Lord, You are God, who made heaven and earth and the sea, and all that is in them. . . . Now, Lord, look on their threats, and grant to Your servants that with all boldness they may speak Your word, by stretching out Your hand to heal, and that signs and wonders may be done through the name of Your holy Servant Jesus.'. . . And when they had prayed, the place where they were assembled together was shaken; and they were all filled with the Holy Spirit, and they spoke the word of God with boldness."

   In whose name did they make their request?

   What was the result of their prayers?

2. **Say in Jesus' Name**

   Not only do we "pray" in Jesus' name, but we can "say"—decree, declare and establish God's will over our lives, families, church and cities—in Jesus' name.

   a. **John 14:12-14**

   "Most assuredly, I say to you, he who believes in Me, the works that I do he will do also; and greater works than these he will do, because I go to My Father. And whatever you ask in My name, that I will do, that the Father may be glorified in the Son. If you ask anything in My name, I will do it."

   To do greater works than Jesus (which is astounding), what must you believe?

   What has Jesus promised to do if you "ask" in His name?

REVELATION DROP: Notice the word *ask* in the context of John 14. Jesus is not referring to prayer as we normally think of it, He's describing the power of "calling for a greater work" to be done in His name for the glory of the Father.[1] This would sound like the very things we see Jesus do when He speaks words to a fig tree, a fever, the wind, and so on. Those are great works! Jesus doesn't pray about the fig tree; He speaks to it with faith-filled words. We also see this done through the disciples in Acts 3. When we *speak, ask, or call* for God's will to be done in Jesus' name for the glory of the Father, Jesus will do it.

What situation in your life, family, or health do you need to call for in Jesus' name? Do you need to *call in* healing restoration? Resurrection of a relationship? Or some other need? (In faith, do it now for the glory of the Father!)

b.　　**Acts 3:6-7**
"Then Peter said, 'Silver and gold I do not have, but what I do have I give you: In the name of Jesus Christ of Nazareth, rise up and walk.' And he took him by the right hand and lifted him up, and immediately his feet and ankle bones received strength."

In whose name do the disciples call for the crippled man to "rise up and walk"?

What happens?

c.　　**Job 22:27-28 AMPC**
"You will make your prayer to Him, and He will hear you, and you will pay your vows. You shall also decide and decree a thing, and it shall be established for you; and the light [of God's favor] shall shine upon your ways."

What will happen when we "decide and decree a thing"?

REVELATION DROP: In prayer, we can decide and decree a thing! Have you "decided and decreed" God's Word lately? It is a good practice to put your voice to your faith in prayer and in declaring God's will. When you decree a thing in Jesus' name, it's like putting a faith stake in the ground and establishing it in your life. God has given you the privilege of deciding and decreeing the will of God over your life every day! It's also a good idea to seek the Lord on what He wants to establish in your life and then make your faith declarations as you are led by the Spirit every year, every month, every week, every day or every hour! It might sound like this, *"Heavenly Father, I pray, decide and decree that this year will be a year of NEW—new doors opened for our family, new depths in prayer for your church, new revelations from Your Word for my husband and I, new favors, new strength, new boldness, new health and new joys! In Jesus' name, I decide and declare these things according to Your Word and by Your Spirit. Amen."*

D. PRAY IN FAITH

I love the testimony of the late missionary evangelist George Mueller, *"I have joyfully dedicated my whole life to the object of exemplifying how much may be accomplished by prayer and faith."* [2]

1. Hebrews 11:6

"But without faith it is impossible to please Him, for he who comes to God must believe that He is, and that He is a rewarder of those who diligently seek Him."

What must you have to please God?

What must you believe to come to God?

What does God do for those who have faith and seek Him?

REVELATION DROP: At first glance, we might think that God is hard to please. In fact, we might think that if we don't have faith, what a disappointment we must be. But that is not what this verse is describing! This passage actually tells us that God is so very pleased when we come to Him in faith to receive all that He has bought and paid for. And He loves to reward those who believe and seek Him. When we don't have faith, we can't receive all that He has provided, and this doesn't please Him. Can you see that? Our faith is released by what we pray and say! This pleases God.

2. Mark 11:22-24

"So Jesus answered and said to them, 'Have faith in God. For assuredly, I say to you, whoever says to this mountain, "Be removed and be cast into the sea," and does not doubt in his heart, but believes that those things he says will be done, he will have whatever he says. Therefore I say to you, whatever things you ask when you pray, believe that you receive them, and you will have them.'"

What are you supposed to "say" and to what?

What are you supposed to believe about what you say?

What are you supposed to "pray" and to whom?

What are you supposed to believe about what you ask?

REVELATION DROP: In this familiar and powerful passage, we see that Jesus wants us to have faith in God. Again, we see that our faith is revealed by what we *say* and *pray*.

>> When it comes to "saying": Once again, we notice the power of our words. We are to speak faith-filled words directly to the things that stand between God's best and us. (Earlier in this passage Jesus speaks directly to a fig tree. Then He tells us to have the same kind of faith!) Three times Jesus talks about what we say, and one time He talks about what we believe. Jesus emphasizes what we say three times more than what we believe. We are to believe the words we speak (decide and decree!) and not doubt. As a result, we will have what we say.

>> When it comes to "praying": Again, we are reminded that there are two tenses when it comes to praying in faith. We pray and believe in the *present tense*, and we shall have in the *future tense*. Jesus tells us to believe we receive whatever we desire when we pray. In other words, in the present tense, when we pray, we should believe we receive the things we ask for. We are to pray and by faith, we are to believe we receive our answer right then. We believe we receive our desire in the present tense, but we shall have it in the future tense. Can you see that?

In other words, we don't believe we receive when we see it; we believe we receive when we pray it. Do you get the distinction? It's a big one! By faith, knowing your desire is in alignment with God's will you believe you receive from God the desire you are praying about. You believe you receive it right then. I'm not going to believe I receive it when I see it, I choose to believe I receive it now, in the present tense. And then in the future tense, you shall see it. You might wonder, how far into the future? That's God's department. It might be in the next three minutes. It might be in the next three years. It might be the next 30 years. The timing on "when we have it" is the Lord's department, but the faith to believe "when we pray" is our department.

3. **Mark 9:23**

   "Jesus said to him, 'If you can believe, all things are possible to him who believes.'"

   What is possible for those who believe?

4. **Matthew 19:26**

   "But Jesus looked at them and said to them, 'With men this is impossible, but with God all things are possible.'"

   What is possible with God?

5. **Luke 1:37**

   "For with God nothing will be impossible."

   What is impossible with God?

REVELATION DROP: Can you see that faith pleases God? Without faith it's impossible to please Him. Everything we do, we are to do by faith. Just as the Bible says, *"The just shall live* *by faith"* (Romans 1:17); when we pray in faith, this pleases God because He knows that faith (what we believe in our heart and say with our mouth) is the secret to receiving anything from Him. If you need more faith, God has told you exactly how to get it: *"So then faith comes by hearing, and hearing by the word of God" (Romans 10:17).*

When it comes to prayer, make sure that you don't pray too hastily. In other words, you want to pray in faith, so you may need to slow down a little bit on the front end and let faith rise in your heart so that when you do pray, you are in faith. You don't get any results from faithless prayers; you just get discouraged.

Be honest with yourself and ask: What do I know about God's will as revealed in His word? Do I believe it? You may know something is God's will, but you may not believe it quite yet. If that is the case, before you pray, take time to meditate on God's Word until you do believe.

I have found that it's better to not pray until I have faith for the thing I am requesting. Instead, I just spend extra time in God's Word, specifically looking up the scriptures that give me the faith I need for the requests I have. For example, if I were praying about finances, I would meditate on numerous scriptures regarding God's will for our finances. If I were praying for healing or wisdom, I would meditate on the scriptures along those lines. Be specific. I know one woman who has believed God's Word and prayed for strong ankle bones. I know another person who prayed and believed God's Word for a fertile and blessed womb. Still another found specific Scriptures about a family move to the south. It's easy to have faith, to pray and believe God for specific things, when you have His specific Word!

However, if your faith isn't where it needs to be, just spend more time in the Word and ask the Lord to fill your heart with the faith that comes from His promises!

E.   PRAY IT OUT

What verse or passages stood out to you in this chapter? What truths stirred your heart?

Take a moment to pray and put these things into practice.

1.   Blue Letter Bible, s.v. "aiteō," March 27, 2021. https://www.blueletterbible.org//lang/lexicon/lexicon.cfm?Strongs=G154&t=KJV.

2.   "George Muller Quotes About Prayer," AZ Quotes, March 26, 2021, https://www.azquotes.com/author/10538-George_Muller/tag/prayer.

CHAPTER 12:

THE "HOW" OF PRAYER - PART 2

"What the church needs today is not machinery or better,
not new organizations or more or novel methods, but men and women
whom the Holy Spirit can use. Men and women mighty in prayer.
The Holy Spirit does not flow through methods but through people of prayer."
E.M. Bounds

Now, let's get down to more nuts and bolts of prayer. How do we pray? More importantly, how do we pray in such a way as to get results? There is nothing worse than praying day after day and year after year and NOT seeing results. In His Word, God specifically tells us He wants us to pray "effectual" prayers—those are the kinds of prayers that get results. But how? How do we pray that way?

>> Is our communication with the Lord supposed to be done in an organic or a systematic way?

>> Is prayer supposed to be the recitation of a memorized protocol or an unrehearsed conversation?

>> Should we pray by just "flowing with the Spirit" as He leads, or should we pray with structure and purpose?

The answer is all of the above!

In other words, praying in both an organic and a systematic way is appropriate. Praying both with memorized prayers and in an unrehearsed way is acceptable. Praying with structure or by simply flowing in the Spirit are both awesome. Prayer is something we do from our heart, not our head. While we use our mind to study the prayer principles in this workbook, God's truths will drop into our hearts, and that is the place from which we pray. It's not enough to know the prayer principles; we must carve out time to pray and develop our relationship with the Lord in the discipline of prayer. Like all things, the only way to get good at something is to practice.

As you can see, communicating with our heavenly Father is a heart-thing, so our prayer life will be unique to each of us. As we talk with the Lord within the boundaries of His Word, we will experience the joy of "effectual" prayers" being answered.

A. PRAY FROM YOUR HEART

As we talk about all the *how's* of prayer, the most important thing is to avoid getting legalistic or feeling that prayer is an obligation, duty, or checklist to complete. Rather, see prayer as the incredible privilege you have to flow in His protocols while talking to God from your heart of hearts. Remember, your prayer life is a wonderful extension of your growing relationship with the Lord.

Charles Spurgeon describes heartfelt prayer in this way, *"True prayer is neither a mere mental exercise nor a vocal performance. It is far deeper than that—it is a spiritual transaction with the Creator of Heaven and Earth."*[1]

We see numerous examples of the effective, heartfelt prayers of many people in the Bible. Let's take a look.

1. **Pray heartfelt prayers like Elijah—James 5:16-18 AMPC.**
   "The earnest (heartfelt, continued) prayer of a righteous man makes tremendous power available [dynamic in its working]. Elijah was a human being with a nature such as we have [with feelings, affections, and a constitution like ours]; and he prayed earnestly for it not to rain, and no rain fell on the earth for three years and six months. And [then] he prayed again and the heavens supplied rain and the land produced its crops [as usual]."

   How do you describe earnest, heartfelt prayers?

2. **Pour out your heart in prayer like David—Psalm 62:8.**
   "Trust in Him at all times, you people; pour out your heart before Him; God is a refuge for us."

   How would you describe what it means to "pour out your heart" before the Lord?

3. **Pray from the depths of your heart like Hannah—1 Samuel 1:10-17.**
   "And she was in bitterness of soul, and prayed to the LORD and wept in anguish. Then she made a vow and said, 'O LORD of hosts, if You will indeed look on the affliction of Your maidservant and remember me, and not forget Your maidservant, but will give Your maidservant a male child, then I will give him to the LORD all the days of his life, and no razor shall come upon his head.'

   "And it happened, as she continued praying before the LORD, that Eli watched her mouth. Now Hannah spoke in her heart; only her lips moved, but her voice was not heard. Therefore Eli thought she was drunk. So Eli said to her, 'How long will you be drunk? Put your wine away from you!' But Hannah answered and said, 'No, my lord, I am a woman of sorrowful spirit. I have drunk neither wine nor intoxicating drink, but have poured out my soul before the LORD. Do not consider your maidservant a wicked woman, for out of the abundance of my complaint and grief I have spoken until now.'

   "Then Eli answered and said, 'Go in peace, and the God of Israel grant your petition which you have asked of Him.' And she said, 'Let your maidservant find favor in your sight.' So the woman went her way and ate, and her face was no longer sad."

   What condition is Hannah in that prompts her to pray?

   How does she pray?

How does God answer her prayer?

How does this make Hannah feel?

4. **Pray from a humble and wise heart like Solomon—1 Kings 3:5-14.**
   "At Gibeon the LORD appeared to Solomon in a dream by night; and God said, 'Ask! What shall I give you?' And Solomon said: 'You have shown great mercy to Your servant David my father, because he walked before You in truth, in righteousness, and in uprightness of heart with You; You have continued this great kindness for him, and You have given him a son to sit on his throne, as it is this day. Now, O LORD my God, You have made Your servant king instead of my father David, but I am a little child; I do not know how to go out or come in. And Your servant is in the midst of Your people whom You have chosen, a great people, too numerous to be numbered or counted. Therefore give to Your servant an understanding heart to judge Your people, that I may discern between good and evil. For who is able to judge this great people of Yours?'

   "The speech pleased the Lord, that Solomon had asked this thing. Then God said to him: 'Because you have asked this thing, and have not asked long life for yourself, nor have asked riches for yourself, nor have asked the life of your enemies, but have asked for yourself understanding to discern justice, behold, I have done according to your words; see, I have given you a wise and understanding heart, so that there has not been anyone like you before you, nor shall any like you arise after you. And I have also given you what you have not asked: both riches and honor, so that there shall not be anyone like you among the kings all your days. So if you walk in My ways, to keep My statutes and My commandments, as your father David walked, then I will lengthen your days.'"

   What does God ask Solomon?

   What does Solomon pray?

   How does God answer?

5. **Pray big prayers like Jabez—1 Chronicles 4:10.**
   "And Jabez called on the God of Israel saying, 'Oh, that You would bless me indeed, and enlarge my territory, that Your hand would be with me, and that You would keep me from evil, that I may not cause pain!' So God granted him what he requested."

   What four things does Jabez request?

   How do you understand Jabez's request that God would "bless him indeed"?

How do you describe Jabez's request that God would "enlarge my territory"?

How do you describe Jabez's request that "God's hand would be with him"?

How do you describe Jabez's request that God would "keep him from evil and not cause pain"?

How does God answer all of Jabez's requests?

6. **Pray with a dedicated heart like Anna—Luke 2:36-38 NLT.**
"Anna, a prophet, was also there in the Temple. She was the daughter of Phanuel from the tribe of Asher, and she was very old. Her husband died when they had been married only seven years. Then she lived as a widow to the age of eighty-four. She never left the Temple but stayed there day and night, worshiping God with fasting and prayer. She came along just as Simeon was talking with Mary and Joseph, and she began praising God. She talked about the child to everyone who had been waiting expectantly for God to rescue Jerusalem."

How does Anna pray?

How does God reward her prayers?

7. **Pray with a glad heart like Mary—Luke 1:45-55.**
"'Blessed is she who believed, for there will be a fulfillment of those things which were told her from the Lord.' And Mary said: 'My soul magnifies the Lord, and my spirit has rejoiced in God my Savior. For He has regarded the lowly state of His maidservant; for behold, henceforth all generations will call me blessed. For He who is mighty has done great things for me, and holy is His name. And His mercy is on those who fear Him From generation to generation. He has shown strength with His arm; He has scattered the proud in the imagination of their hearts. He has put down the mighty from their thrones, and exalted the lowly. He has filled the hungry with good things, and the rich He has sent away empty. He has helped His servant Israel, in remembrance of His mercy, as He spoke to our fathers, to Abraham and to his seed forever.'"

How does Mary pray after she receives the promise from God?

B. HOW NOT TO PRAY

Have you ever wondered why some prayers seem to get answered and other prayers don't seem to reach heaven? Here are some things to consider.

1. **Don't pray like a hypocrite—Matthew 6:5.**
"And when you pray, you shall not be like the hypocrites. For they love to pray standing in the

synagogues and on the corners of the streets, that they may be seen by men. Assuredly, I say to you, they have their reward."

How do hypocrites pray?

2. **Don't pray with vain repetitions—Matthew 6:6-8.**
    "But you, when you pray, go into your room, and when you have shut your door, pray to your Father who is in the secret place; and your Father who sees in secret will reward you openly. And when you pray, do not use vain repetitions as the heathen do. For they think that they will be heard for their many words. Therefore do not be like them."

What does it sound like to pray vain repetitions with many words?

REVELATION DROP: We don't have to repeat ourselves over and over. Sometimes we think the more words we use to pray, the better, but God can answer short faith-filled prayers just as easily as repetitive, drawn-out prayers. It's also easy to get into the mindless habit of using God's name in vain by saying certain Christian prayer clichés over and over while praying like: Hallelujah. Glory to God. Praise the Lord. Heavenly Father, or Father God. Of course, all of these phrases have their place, and when spoken from the heart, they are very powerful; but we shouldn't overuse these kinds of words as vain repetitions.

3. **Don't pray in unbelief—James 1:5-8.**
    "If any of you lacks wisdom, let him ask of God, who gives to all liberally and without reproach, and it will be given to him. But let him ask in faith, with no doubting, for he who doubts is like a wave of the sea driven and tossed by the wind. For let not that man suppose that he will receive anything from the Lord; he is a double-minded man, unstable in all his ways."

If you lack wisdom (or anything else!), what should you do?

What does God want to do?

How should you ask?

According to verses 6-7, what will the person who doubts receive?

REVELATION DROP: An effective prayer life is based upon faith. As we can see, doubt causes us to be double-minded, unstable, and unable to receive answers to our prayer. Faith gives us a single-minded confidence in God's ability and willingness to answer our prayers.

4. **Don't pray with unforgiveness in your heart—Mark 11:25.**

"And whenever you stand praying, if you have anything against anyone, forgive him, that your Father in heaven may also forgive you your trespasses."

If you have anything against anyone, what should you do?

5. **Don't pray from a prideful position—Luke 18:9-14.**

"Also He spoke this parable to some who trusted in themselves that they were righteous, and despised others: 'Two men went up to the temple to pray, one a Pharisee and the other a tax collector. The Pharisee stood and prayed thus with himself, "God, I thank You that I am not like other men—extortioners, unjust, adulterers, or even as this tax collector. I fast twice a week; I give tithes of all that I possess." And the tax collector, standing afar off, would not so much as raise his eyes to heaven, but beat his breast, saying, "God, be merciful to me a sinner!" I tell you, this man went down to his house justified rather than the other; for everyone who exalts himself will be humbled, and he who humbles himself will be exalted.'"

What two people go to pray?

What does the Pharisee pray?

What does the tax collector pray?

Whose prayer pleases the Lord?

What is promised to the humble person?

REVELATION DROP: When we pray, we should not be prideful or self-righteous. We should also be aware of "teaching God or others" when we pray. Have you ever prayed or heard someone pray like this: *"Dear Father, we know that You are a God who answers prayers of faith, and we know that faith in the Greek and Hebrew is what we believe in our hearts and say with our mouths. In the Amplified Bible, we can see that unbelief will short circuit our prayers, so dear Father, we should always spend time hearing and hearing God's Word to grow our faith, and if we want to pray effectively . . . "* And the next thing you know, you've gone into a teaching prayer! Teaching is good and needful, but not while we are praying. Stay humble and remember, prayer is a heartfelt, faith-filled conversation with the Lord, not a theological teaching.

The way Charles Finney puts it will put a smile on your face, *"Some men will spin out a long prayer telling God who and what He is, or they pray out a whole system of divinity. Some people preach, others exhort the people, till everybody wishes they would stop, and God wishes so, too, most undoubtedly."*[2]

6. **Don't pray and give up—Luke 18:1-8.**

"Then He spoke a parable to them, that men always ought to pray and not lose heart, saying: 'There was in a certain city a judge who did not fear God nor regard man. Now there was a widow in that city; and she came to him, saying, "Get justice for me from my adversary." And he would not for a while; but afterward he said within himself, "Though I do not fear God nor regard man, yet because this widow troubles me I will avenge her, lest by her continual coming she weary me."' Then the Lord said, 'Hear what the unjust judge said. And shall God not avenge His own elect who cry out day and night to Him, though He bears long with them? I tell you that He will avenge them speedily. Nevertheless, when the Son of Man comes, will He really find faith on the earth?'"

What should you always do, and what should you not do?

Describe the widow's persistence.

How does this translate into your prayer life?

REVELATION DROP: Once we pray, we don't need to keep asking for the same thing over and over, but we can remind and thank the Lord over and over! In other words, we ask and request once, and if we believe we have received it, we thank the Lord for His answer until it is manifested. We don't grow impatient or give up; rather, while we are exercising our faith and patience, we remind and thank Him for the answer day and night. God always answers faith-filled prayers that are according to His Word, but answers don't always come immediately. That's why fruitful, faith-filled prayer requires patience, perseverance, and a thankful heart.

7. **Don't pray with selfish motives—James 4:1-3.**

"Where do wars and fights come from among you? Do they not come from your desires for pleasure that war in your members? You lust and do not have. You murder and covet and cannot obtain. You fight and war. Yet you do not have because you do not ask. You ask and do not receive, because you ask amiss, that you may spend it on your pleasures."

Why do you not have things you desire?

Why do you ask and not receive the things you desire?

REVELATION DROP: When we pray, our motives must be in agreement with God and His Word. God does not answer prayers that go against His character. He will not answer prayers that are motivated by selfish, carnal desires, but rather He hears and answers prayers that further His purpose in our lives. Always pray with a desire to live your life and receive answers to your prayers that are pleasing to the Lord.

C. PRAY IT OUT

What verse or passages stood out to you in this chapter? What truths stirred your heart?

Take a moment to pray and put these things into practice.

1. "Charles Spurgeon Quotes," Brainy Quote, May 1, 2021, https://www.brainyquote.com/quotes/charles_spurgeon_718699.

2. "Charles Finney Quotes," Christian Quotes, May 5, 2021, https://www.christianquotes.info/quotes-by-author/charles-finney-quotes/.

CHAPTER 13

THE "HOW" OF PRAYER - PART 3

"Groanings which cannot be uttered are often prayers which cannot be refused."
Charles Spurgeon

God is so good! He's given us many ways to pray. Do you remember why? The Lord wants our joy to be full. Jesus tells us, *"Most assuredly, I say to you, whatever you ask the Father in My name He will give you. Until now you have asked nothing in My name. Ask, and you will receive, that your joy may be full" (John 16:23,24).* I hope that your study in *Getting a Grip on the Basics of Prayer* is increasing your faith and joy!

As we continue in our study on "how" to pray, let's look at two ways we can pray every day.

>> We can *pray with our understanding.*
>> We can *pray with our spirit.*

A.   PRAY IN TWO WAYS

In prayer, we are the *followers*, not the *leaders*. This is an important distinction. As it turns out, prayer is not only talking to God—it is listening first and then talking. In prayer, we follow the Lord's leading. In prayer, we follow Him to pray "with our understanding" and/or "with the spirit." Let's take a look.

1.   **1 Corinthians 14:15**
        "What is the conclusion then? I will pray with the spirit, and I will also pray with the understanding. I will sing with the spirit, and I will also sing with the understanding."

        What two ways can you pray and sing?

        What do you think it means to "pray/sing with the spirit"?

        What do you think it means to "pray/sing with the understanding"?

        REVELATION DROP: Can you see that there are two ways to pray? We can pray "with our understanding" and "with the spirit." The Amplified Bible, Classic Edition helps us to see this verse more clearly: *"Then what am I to do? I will pray with my spirit [by the Holy Spirit that is within me], but I will also pray [intelligently] with my mind and understanding; I will sing with my spirit [by the Holy Spirit that is within me], but I will sing [intelligently] with my mind and* *understanding also."*

Notice that when we "pray with my spirit [by the Holy Spirit that is within me]"—it is from our spirit (or heart) that we pray, and the Holy Spirit is initiating, helping, prompting, and guiding us. We can pray this way in both our native known language, as well as, in our spiritual language of tongues.

When we "pray with our understanding," we are praying intelligently with our mind and understanding. We pray this way in our native known language.

2. **Ephesians 6:18**
    "Praying always with all prayer and supplication in the Spirit, being watchful to this end with all perseverance and supplication for all the saints."

    How are we to pray always?

    How would you describe "in the Spirit"?

    What does it mean to "be watchful"?

    REVELATION DROP: It's important to always pray all of our prayers "in the Spirit"—from our spirit and being led by the Holy Spirit. That means we "pray with our understanding" in the Spirit, and we "pray with the spirit" in the Spirit! Do you see the distinction?

    Being "watchful" in prayer is an important ingredient for being led by the Spirit. Let's look at this further.

3. **1 Peter 4:7**
    "But the end of all things is at hand; therefore be serious and watchful in your prayers."

    In what way should you pray?

    REVELATION DROP: To be "sober and watchful" is to be in our right mind, awake, and alert in prayer. This is a very important aspect of prayer as it helps us to follow the Lord and His leadings, rather than our own thoughts and emotions.

    In the Old Testament, watchmen would be assigned to guard the city by standing upon the city walls to scan the horizon and watch for intruders. They would sound the alarm as needed to protect their city.

    Habakkuk was describing the role of a watchmen as it related to his relationship with the Lord. As a watchman in prayer, he looked and listened to hear from God, and then he responded: *"I will climb up to my watchtower and stand at my guardpost. There I will wait to see what the*

LORD says" (Habakkuk 2:1 NLT).

Watching has various meanings, and this is something we can do intentionally. Here are a few examples:

>> We can guard and protect people in prayer, just as the shepherds did when they "kept watch" over their sheep (Luke 2:8).

>> We can keep awake and be vigilant in prayer, just as Jesus told us to "watch and pray" so that we do not enter into temptation (Mark 14:38).

>> We can prayerfully discern the signs of the times, just as Jesus told us about the time of His return and the importance of taking heed to "watch and pray" (Mark 13:33).

>> We can watch and pray over the spiritual condition of those in our care, just as the writer of Hebrews told the spiritual leaders to "watch for the souls" in their care (Hebrews 13:17).

In prayer, we, too, can "watch" to see what the Holy Spirit reveals, shows, and speaks to us; and then we can respond by praying "with our understanding" and "with our spirit." In this spiritual discipline of watching, the Lord will allow us to "see" with the eyes of our heart and to "know" what we need to know to follow Him in prayer. It may be as you "watch," that you'll have a "knowing" that you should pray for a particular person or situation, or it may be that the Lord will allow you to "see" a particular thing that needs prayer, or He may speak a word to your heart that will prompt you to pray. Follow His lead.

Now, let's look at how to "pray with your understanding" and how to "pray with your spirit" in more detail.

B. PRAY WITH YOUR UNDERSTANDING

To pray "with your understanding" is to pray intelligently with your renewed mind as you are led by the Spirit. When you pray this way, you pray in our known language based upon the knowledge you have as well as by the leadings and promptings of the Spirit. You pray "with your understanding" when you pray the Word, when you pray any of the prayers in the Bible, and when you pray based upon the revelation God has given you.

For most people, praying "with their understanding" is the primary way they pray. The Apostle Paul prayed "with his understanding" for believers in the various New Testament churches. I love reading his prayers found in Ephesians 1, Ephesians 3, Colossians 1 and Philippians 1. While we were in Bible college, one of our mentors highly encouraged us to pray these prayers and when I think about the way the Lord has led me to pray for my husband, our kids, grandkids, extended family (every blood, step-, and in-law relative), and our church family; I realize that I have prayed the same prayers the Apostle Paul prayed (listed below) more than any other single prayer. In doing so, I know I am praying according to God's will because these prayers are based in His Word. When I pray these prayers, I insert the names of those for whom I am praying, and I pray with my understanding. You can too! I encourage you pray the following prayers on a regular basis for yourself and your family and friends.

119

1. **Pray for the spirit of revelation—Ephesians 1:15-19 NLT.**
    "Therefore I also, after I heard of your faith in the Lord Jesus and your love for all the saints, do not cease to give thanks for you, making mention of you in my prayers: that the God of our Lord Jesus Christ, the Father of glory, may give to you the spirit of wisdom and revelation in the knowledge of Him, the eyes of your understanding being enlightened; that you may know what is the hope of His calling, what are the riches of the glory of His inheritance in the saints, and what is the exceeding greatness of His power toward us who believe."

    What specific things did the Apostle Paul ask the Lord to give to these believers?

    How would this prayer sound with your name (or a loved one) into every line? (Write it out.)

    REVELATION DROP: This is a great template for "praying with your understanding." Notice all of the things the Apostle Paul prayed for. He wasn't inventing things to ask for; rather, he was appropriating the blessings that already belonged to him and all believers. He prayed for a greater manifestation of wisdom, revelation, enlightenment, power, and the riches of Christ to be given to the believers.

2. **Pray for a revelation of His love—Ephesians 3:14-21.**
    "For this reason I bow my knees to the Father of our Lord Jesus Christ, from whom the whole family in heaven and earth is named, that He would grant you, according to the riches of His glory, to be strengthened with might through His Spirit in the inner man, that Christ may dwell in your hearts through faith; that you, being rooted and grounded in love, may be able to comprehend with all the saints what is the width and length and depth and height—to know the love of Christ which passes knowledge; that you may be filled with all the fullness of God. Now to Him who is able to do exceedingly abundantly above all that we ask or think, according to the power that works in us, to Him be glory in the church by Christ Jesus to all generations, forever and ever. Amen."

    How would this prayer sound with your name inserted into it? (Go ahead and write out this prayer with your name in it. Now, pray what you have written word-for-word to the Father.)

3. **Pray for a life pleasing to the Lord—Colossians 1:9-12 NLT.**
    "So we have not stopped praying for you since we first heard about you. We ask God to give you complete knowledge of His will and to give you spiritual wisdom and understanding. Then the way you live will always honor and please the Lord, and your lives will produce every kind of good fruit. All the while, you will grow as you learn to know God better and better. We also pray that you will be strengthened with all His glorious power so you will have all the endurance and patience you need. May you be filled with joy, always thanking the Father."

    Describe the things the Apostle Paul prayed for in this prayer:

REVELATION DROP: I believe that one of the things that contributed to the spiritual growth and development of our family and our church family has been praying these Scriptural prayers and inserting the names of individuals into them on a regular basis.

As we were raising our kids, this prayer became a cornerstone in our family. We prayed then and we pray now that God would fill us with the knowledge of His will with all spiritual wisdom and understanding. We pray that He helps us to stay out of the ditch of legalistic, religious bondage and out of the ditch of free-wheeling sin, and that He helps us to live a life that honors and pleases Him. We know this is what will produce every kind of good fruit.

There is one other thing that is very important in this prayer. Notice that as Christians, we are to live a life filled with joy. Joy is the distinguishing characteristic of a Christian. No one wants to be the non-joyful Christian—the stern, mean, stoic, angry, self-righteous, complaining, grumbling, murmuring Christian; but if we aren't prayerful, we can become just that. God's plan is for us to pray for one another so that we are filled with joy and gratitude.

4. **Pray for God's best spirit, soul and body—3 John 1:2.**
   "Beloved, I pray that you may prosper in all things and be in health, just as your soul prospers."

How can you *pray with your understanding* for prosperity in all things? (spirit)

How can you *pray with your understanding* for prosperity in all things? (soul)

How can you *pray with your understanding* for your health? (body)

REVELATION DROP: I know a woman who "prays with her understanding" regarding her health. She received a diagnosis of early stage osteoporosis, but she knows God's Word is the final authority. A friend of hers, who happens to be a faith-filled Christian and an orthopedic surgeon, encouraged her to pray according to the medical knowledge he shared with her. So, in addition to being led by the Spirit in her diet and exercise, she shared that she prays this way, *"I pray with my understanding according to knowledge and I rebuke osteoporosis. I call in the healing restoration and resurrection of bone metabolism. I rebuke the osteoclasts dominance over the osteoblasts, and I ask the Lord, as my Creator, to energize the osteoblast bone formation via the stimulation of IGF-1, the local growth hormone. I ask this in Jesus' name. amen."* In addition, every day she and her husband call her bones "strong!"

What knowledge do you have about the things you are praying about? Use that knowledge to "pray with your understanding" for the prosperity of your life spirit, soul and body.

Now, let's look at how to "pray with your spirit."

C. PRAY WITH YOUR SPIRIT

Pierre Teilhard de Chardin said, *"We are not human beings having a spiritual experience. We are spiritual beings having a human experience."*[1] How true this is, and prayer brings this to the forefront.

1. **Pray in Tongues**

   In this section, let's focus on "praying with our spirit" in tongues (with our spiritual prayer language) in our private prayer life. *Praying* with your spirit in other tongues is distinctly different from the public gift of *speaking* in tongues. *Praying* in the spirit in tongues is quite literally—a prayer! *Speaking* in tongues is literally—speaking a message, which requires an interpretation (1 Corinthians 14).

   a. **1 Corinthians 14:14-15**

   "For if I pray in a tongue, my spirit prays, but my understanding is unfruitful. What is the conclusion then? I will pray with the spirit, and I will also pray with the understanding. I will sing with the spirit, and I will also sing with the understanding."

   When you pray in tongues, what part of you is praying?

   When you pray in tongues, what part of you is unfruitful?

   REVELATION DROP: I like how the Classic Amplified Bible reads, *"For if I pray in an [unknown] tongue, my spirit [by the Holy Spirit within me] prays, but my mind is unproductive [it bears no fruit and helps nobody]. Then what am I to do? I will pray with my spirit [by the Holy Spirit that is within me], but I will also pray [intelligently] with my mind and understanding; I will sing with my spirit [by the Holy Spirit that is within me], but I will sing [intelligently] with my mind and understanding also."* Do you see the distinction between your spirit and the Holy Spirit within you? When we pray in tongues, our spirit does the praying, empowered by the Holy Spirit with words that He gives us.

   b. **1 Corinthians 14:2**

   "For he who speaks in a tongue does not speak to men but to God, for no one understands him; however, in the spirit he speaks mysteries."

   When you speak in tongues in this way, who are you speaking to?

   Who are you *not* speaking to when you speak/pray in tongues?

   When you speak in tongues, what are you speaking?

   REVELATION DROP: When we are speaking in tongues to God (as distinct from speaking in tongues for the congregation to hear,) and this is another way of saying we are praying in tongues. When we do so, we are speaking mysteries. When you think about it, most everything in our lives is a mystery. None of us know the future, so everything about our future is a mystery. The way things will come together to fit into God's perfect plan is often a mystery. Who we will marry may be a mystery. The destiny God has for our children is a mystery. And on it goes.

Our understanding doesn't know what we are praying about, but our spirit is flowing with the Holy Spirit to pray according to God's will. When we pray in tongues, we have the ability to pray about those mysteries and we can "pray ahead." When we speak to God in tongues, we pray out mysteries, and we "lay the track" that we will walk on as we eventually step into our future.

I believe this is one of the greatest prayer privileges God has given us. In my own life, I have found great peace and comfort in praying this way for my future, my marriage, my family, each one of our children, our church family, and most anything else the Lord puts on my heart. I encourage you to set aside time to simply pray in tongues as a means of praying out the mysteries God has planned for you and others.

c. **1 Corinthians 14:4 NLT**
"A person who speaks in tongues is strengthened personally, but one who speaks a word of prophecy strengthens the entire church."

Who gets strengthened by praying in the private practice of speaking in tongues (inspired words spoken in an unknown language)?

Who gets strengthened by the public demonstration of prophecy (inspired words in a known language)?

d. **1 Corinthians 14:13**
"Therefore let him who speaks in a tongue pray that he may interpret."

When you speak in tongues, what else can you pray for?

REVELATION DROP: When you are speaking (or praying) in tongues in your private life, since your understanding will not know what you are praying about, you can ask the Lord to help you interpret (to have revelation on) what you are praying.

e. **Jude 1:20**
"But you, beloved, building yourselves up on your most holy faith, praying in the Holy Spirit."

According to this passage, how should you pray?

What does this accomplish?

REVELATION DROP: Did you know that you can build up your life in Christ by praying in the Spirit? Do you need to "build" yourself up spiritually? Emotionally? Physically? Then pray!

You don't have to wait for a special feeling or "holy goosebumps" to pray in tongues; you can simply choose to do it. Just like turning the water on and off at your faucet, you can turn your spirit on and open your mouth. Trust the Holy Spirit to give you the utterance in tongues to pray. In the same way that there is water in the pipes at home and water comes out when you turn the faucet on; so, too, the Holy Spirit fills you and when you turn on your spirit man to pray, your heavenly language will come out! When you pray in the Spirit, in tongues, you are building yourself up.

f.   **1 Corinthians 2:9-13**

"But as it is written: 'Eye has not seen, nor ear heard, nor have entered into the heart of man The things which God has prepared for those who love Him.' But God has revealed them to us through His Spirit. For the Spirit searches all things, yes, the deep things of God. For what man knows the things of a man except the spirit of the man which is in him? Even so no one knows the things of God except the Spirit of God. Now we have received, not the spirit of the world, but the Spirit who is from God, that we might know the things that have been freely given to us by God. These things we also speak, not in words which man's wisdom teaches but which the Holy Spirit teaches, comparing spiritual things with spiritual."

What have your eyes, ears, and heart not seen, heard, or understood?

What has God revealed by His Spirit to your spirit?

How do you pray about the things God reveals?

REVELATION DROP: This is a meaty passage about our present and our future and the power of speaking Spirit-empowered words. Our eyes, ears, and minds cannot conceive of the things God has prepared for those who love Him. However, the Spirit has revealed the things God has prepared for us. How do those things become real in our lives? We speak of these things in words which the Holy Spirit gives us—other tongues—and as we speak and pray in the spirit, we gain more revelation on the things God has prepared for us! What a wonderful gift to be able to pray with our spirit.

2.   **Pray in Groanings**

Not only has God given us the ability to pray in the spiritual language of other tongues, He has given us the ability to pray with groanings by the power of the Holy Spirit.

124

"Likewise the Spirit also helps in our weaknesses. For we do not know what we should pray for as we ought, but the Spirit Himself makes intercession for us with groanings which cannot be uttered. Now He who searches the hearts knows what the mind of the Spirit is, because He makes intercession for the saints according to the will of God. And we know that all things work together for good to those who love God, to those who are the called according to His purpose."

Who helps you in your weaknesses when you don't know how to pray as you ought?

How does the Holy Spirit help you?

After you have prayed in this way, what do you know?

REVELATION DROP: Have you ever wanted to pray for God's perfect will to be done in your life, but you just didn't know how to pray? That's where the Holy Spirit comes in. When we don't know what to pray as we ought (which is quite often), the Holy Spirit will help us pray according to God's perfect will.

In this passage, there are two key words we want to focus on: *weakness* and *groanings*.

When we have a weakness, the Holy Spirit helps us to pray in heartfelt groanings. So, what does it mean to have a weakness? What are groanings?

>> **Weakness:** The word *weakness* in the New King James Bible is the same word as *infirmities* from the King James Bible. These words are from the Greek word *astheneia*. The Biblical uses of this Greek word include: "feebleness of health or sickness of body as well as, a want of strength indicating an inability to produce results in our mind or soul."[2]

In other words, when we have an inability to produce results in our lives, whether it's a feebleness, a physical sickness, a mental or emotional issue, or the inability to produce results in any area of our life—the Holy Spirit will help us pray. He always prays according to the will of God, so it is in our best interests to pray with groanings when we have a weakness.

>> **Groanings:** One meaning of the phrase "groanings which cannot be uttered" according to the *Jameison-Faussett-Brown Commentary* is *"that is which cannot be expressed in articulate language."*[3] In other words, to pray with groanings is a heartfelt spiritual transaction, and these groanings can be in a language which our intellect doesn't normally articulate—that is, groans and other tongues.

So then, when we have a weakness—any feebleness, sickness, or inability to produce results—the Holy Spirit will help us to pray with groanings (like a woman giving birth) to bring forth God's will in our lives. When we yield to the Holy Spirit in this way, He will take hold of the weakness we face (our inability to produce results), and He will help us to pray in a way we cannot express in articulate language—with groanings and in tongues—

which will bring forth God's will. As a result, we can rest in knowing that all things will work together for our good and God's purpose (Romans 8:28).

In my experience, when I have had a weakness, and I haven't known what to pray, the practice of yielding to the Holy Spirit to pray from my spirit in tongues or groanings has given me the ability to pray according to His perfect will.

Perhaps you have a weakness—an inability to produce results—in your life. Why not set aside time to pray this way? Simply yield to the Spirit and follow His prompting as you pray in tongues and groanings. The secret to praying in tongues is to quiet your mind and follow the Holy Spirit from your spirit. We don't have to lead or try to think about what to pray; we simply follow His lead and yield to praying out whatever words seem pleasant. It may seem pleasant to pray in tongues softly or loudly or in an authoritative way. Or, it may seem pleasant to simply groan within your spirit. Just flow with His lead, and you'll have a divine experience in prayer.

When you pray in groanings and tongues in the Spirit, He may lead you to pray for your neighbor, an old classmate, or a Gospel breakthrough in the Middle East. Your understanding may not know all the details, but you can rest in knowing that you are praying according to His perfect will, and He will cause all things to work together for good for those who love Him and are called to His purpose. It's an adventure to pray this way!

I hope you are getting stirred up to set aside some time, whether kneeling by your bed, driving in your car, on a train commute, while the kids nap, or when going for a walk to pray in your known language and to pray in tongues and groanings.

There is so much more to know and experience when it comes to praying this way, so if this is a new topic for you, again, I encourage you to review our *Getting a Grip on the Basics* workbook or our *Spirit-Empowered Life* online course where we go into more details on being filled with the Spirit and praying in tongues and groanings.

D. PRAY IT OUT

What verse or passages stood out to you in this chapter? What truths stirred your heart?

Take a moment to pray and put these things into practice.

1. "Pierre Teilhard de Chardin Quotes," Brain Quote, May 20, 2021, https://www.brainyquote.com/quotes/pierre_teilhard_de_chardi_160888.

2. Blue Letter Bible, s.v. "Astheneia," May 2, 2021, https://www.blueletterbible.org//lang/lexicon/lexicon.cfm?Strongs=G769&t=KJV.

3. Robert Jamieson, D.D, A.R. Faussett, and David Brown, "Commentary on Romans 8:26," studylight.org, May 17, 2021, https://www.studylight.org/commentaries/jfb/romans-8.html.

SECTION 6:

THE "WHEN" OF PRAYER

CHAPTER 14:

THE "WHEN" OF PRAYER

"Work, work, from morning until late at night.
In fact, I have so much to do that I shall have to spend the first three hours in prayer."
Martin Luther

When should we pray? How long is long enough? How short is too short? The truth is we can pray at any time for as long as we like. God is all-powerful, all-knowing, and present everywhere at all times.

A. PRAY ALWAYS

1 Thessalonians 5:17-18 MSG
"Be cheerful no matter what; pray all the time; thank God no matter what happens. This is the way God wants you who belong to Christ Jesus to live."

Even if you don't feel cheerful, what should you do?

Even if the "Spirit doesn't move you," when should you pray?

Even if you don't feel thankful, what should you do?

REVELATION DROP: Praying at all times includes praying about big and little things. You can pray about something as little as finding your keys, getting a good parking spot, or having favor with the waitress; and you can pray about something as large as praying for wisdom for government leaders, for God's will to be done in world events or for God's wisdom to increase your income. To pray all the time doesn't mean you cannot do anything else; after all, God knows you have to eat, sleep, work, and engage in relationships with your family and friends. We can always pray by keeping our spiritual radar tuned into God and having an ongoing awareness and internal conversation with Him. So, let's look at when we should pray.

B. PRAY WHEN THE SPIRIT MOVES YOU

Always pray when the Spirit moves you. Being Spirit-led is essential in prayer. Often the Holy Spirit will give us a prompting or an unction to pray. It may be as simple as God's still small voice bringing someone you have not thought about in a long time across your mind and heart. Take those cues as a prompting from the Spirit to pray. It may be that the Holy Spirit quickens your heart with His wisdom or a warning. It's good to take that as His signal to pray. It may be that the Holy Spirit will give you a dream to prompt you to pray to either change or prepare for what is to come. In other words, there are numerous ways the Holy Spirit leads us to pray.

The first mention of prayer after Jesus' resurrection and as the early church began is found in Acts 1 when 120 disciples are instructed on when and where to gather together for prayer. It's evident the early church was led by the Spirit and knew when to pray.

1. **Pray when compassion moves you—Matthew 9:36-39.**
    Then Jesus went about all the cities and villages, teaching in their synagogues, preaching the gospel of the kingdom, and healing every sickness and every disease among the people. But when He saw the multitudes, He was moved with compassion for them, because they were weary and scattered, like sheep having no shepherd. Then He said to His disciples, "The harvest truly is plentiful, but the laborers are few. Therefore pray the Lord of the harvest to send out laborers into His harvest."

    What moved Jesus?

    As a result, what did He tell His disciples (and us) to pray for?

2. **Pray when the Lord asks you to pray—Acts 1:12-14.**
    "Then they returned to Jerusalem from the mount called Olivet, which is near Jerusalem, a Sabbath day's journey. And when they had entered, they went up into the upper room where they were staying: Peter, James, John, and Andrew; Philip and Thomas; Bartholomew and Matthew; James the son of Alphaeus and Simon the Zealot; and Judas the son of James. These all continued with one accord in prayer and supplication, with the women and Mary the mother of Jesus, and with His brothers."

    What did the early church do when they gathered in one accord?

    REVELATION DROP: These believers were led by the Spirit to be in the right place at the right time. They set aside their own agendas and were in one accord. Have you ever thought about what the early church might have looked like if the believers had not followed the Lord's prompting to meet and pray? It turns out that at this Day of Pentecost prayer meeting, the Church was launched! Have you ever considered what might be launched when you gather to pray?

3. **Pray as the Spirit leads you—Romans 8:14 NLT.**
    "For all who are led by the Spirit of God are children of God."

    What does the Spirit of God do in your life?

C. PRAY WHEN THE SPIRIT DOESN'T MOVE YOU

Often, our Christian life is less about what we feel and more about what we know. The discipline of prayer is something we do because we know of its importance and the benefits of doing so. You may not always "feel" a prompting from the Holy Spirit, but that doesn't mean you cannot or should not pray. When it comes to prayer, if we don't sense the Spirit moving us, we can and should pray as an obedient discipline simply because the Lord has asked us to do so. We should pray in agreement with God's Word and His desire to see His will done on earth as it is in heaven. Often, we may get started in prayer as an act of faith, but as we pray, our feelings will catch up and we will sense the Holy Spirit's presence and leading. Let's take a look.

1. **Pray when you feel anxious—Philippians 4:6.**
   "Be anxious for nothing, but in everything by prayer and supplication, with thanksgiving, let your requests be made known to God."

   What do you do when you feel anxious?

   What attitude should you always add to your prayers?

2. **Pray when your enemies threaten you—Psalm 18:3.**
   "I call upon the Lord, who is worthy to be praised, and I am saved from my enemies."

   In what way can you pray when enemies are coming against you?

3. **Pray when you need to forgive someone—Luke 23:33-34 NLT.**
   "When they came to a place called The Skull, they nailed Him to the cross. And the criminals were also crucified—one on His right and one on His left. Jesus said, 'Father, forgive them, for they don't know what they are doing.'"

   Who does Jesus pray for?

   How does Jesus pray for the criminals on His right and left?

   REVELATION DROP: If you need to forgive someone, remember the way Jesus prayed. He asked the Father to forgive them. Sometimes you may not feel you have it within yourself to forgive someone for the wrong they have inflicted, but when you can't seem to forgive, you can ask the Father to forgive them.

4. **Pray when you have tears—Psalm 56:8,10 NCV.**
   "You have recorded my troubles. You have kept a list of my tears. Aren't they in your records? . . . I praise God for His word to me; I praise the Lord for His word."

What type of prayer should you pray when you have troubles and tears?

What moves you to prayerful tears? Personal troubles? Compassion for others? Other?

5. **Pray when you are tempted to be shaken—Psalm 62:5-6,8 NLT.**
"Let all that I am wait quietly before God, for my hope is in Him. He alone is my rock and my salvation, my fortress where I will not be shaken. . . . O my people, trust in Him at all times. Pour out your heart to Him, for God is our refuge."

How do you pray when you are being shaken?

What does it mean to pour out your heart to Him?

How do you pour out your heart to the Lord in faith rather than in fear?

6. **Pray when you say goodbye—Acts 20:31-38.**
"Therefore watch, and remember that for three years I did not cease to warn everyone night and day with tears. 'So now, brethren, I commend you to God and to the word of His grace, which is able to build you up and give you an inheritance among all those who are sanctified. I have coveted no one's silver or gold or apparel. Yes, you yourselves know that these hands have provided for my necessities, and for those who were with me. I have shown you in every way, by laboring like this, that you must support the weak. And remember the words of the Lord Jesus, that He said, "It is more blessed to give than to receive."' And when he had said these things, he knelt down and prayed with them all. Then they all wept freely, and fell on Paul's neck and kissed him, sorrowing most of all for the words which he spoke, that they would see his face no more. And they accompanied him to the ship."

What should you do when you say goodbye to those you love?

D.   PRAY WHEN YOU WANT TO

1. **Pray whenever you want to talk to God—Psalm 27:7-8 NLT.**
"Hear me as I pray, O Lord. Be merciful and answer me! My heart has heard You say, 'Come and talk with me.' And my heart responds, 'Lord, I am coming.'"

What does your heart hear God say?

How should you respond?

2. **Pray when you want God's presence—Exodus 33:12-23.**

"One day Moses said to the LORD, 'You have been telling me, "Take these people up to the Promised Land." But You haven't told me whom You will send with me. You have told me, "I know you by name, and I look favorably on you." If it is true that you look favorably on me, let me know Your ways so I may understand You more fully and continue to enjoy Your favor. And remember that this nation is Your very own people.' The LORD replied, 'I will personally go with you, Moses, and I will give you rest—everything will be fine for you.' Then Moses said, 'If You don't personally go with us, don't make us leave this place. How will anyone know that You look favorably on me—on me and on Your people—if You don't go with us? For Your presence among us sets Your people and me apart from all other people on the earth.' The LORD replied to Moses, 'I will indeed do what you have asked, for I look favorably on you, and I know you by name.' Moses responded, 'Then show me Your glorious presence.' The LORD replied, 'I will make all My goodness pass before you, and I will call out My name, Yahweh, before you. For I will show mercy to anyone I choose, and I will show compassion to anyone I choose. But you may not look directly at My face, for no one may see Me and live.' The LORD continued, 'Look, stand near Me on this rock. As My glorious presence passes by, I will hide you in the crevice of the rock and cover you with My hand until I have passed by. Then I will remove My hand and let you see Me from behind. But my face will not be seen.'"

What does Moses request of the Lord? (List everything you see.)

What does God do for Moses?

REVELATION DROP: Isn't this a wonderful and interesting conversation between God and Moses? Communication with God is prayer. Notice, Moses asked for God's *presence*, and God answered with His *goodness*. God equated His presence with His goodness. Isn't that so good? That means when we experience God's goodness in our lives, that IS a manifestation of His presence. Under the New Covenant, God's presence is with us all of the time because Jesus said that He would never leave us or forsake us. He also told us God is a good Father who gives good gifts to His children. Keep these things in mind the next time you pray for a fresh awareness of God's presence in your life.

3. **Pray when you need wisdom—James 1:5-8.**

"If any of you lacks wisdom, let him ask of God, who gives to all liberally and without reproach, and it will be given to him. But let him ask in faith, with no doubting, for he who doubts is like a wave of the sea driven and tossed by the wind. For let not that man suppose that he will receive anything from the Lord; he is a double-minded man, unstable in all his ways."

What can you do when you need wisdom?

How should you ask for wisdom?

What role does doubt play, and what are the results?

133

4. **Pray when you are in distress—Psalm 118:5-6.**
   "In my distress I prayed to the Lord, and the Lord answered me and set me free. The Lord is for me, so I will have no fear. What can mere people do to me?"

   What does the Lord do when we pray this way?

   Who is for you?

   What can mere people do to you?

5. **Pray when you are sick or suffering—James 5:13-18.**
   "Is anyone among you suffering? Let him pray. Is anyone cheerful? Let him sing psalms. Is anyone among you sick? Let him call for the elders of the church, and let them pray over him, anointing him with oil in the name of the Lord. And the prayer of faith will save the sick, and the Lord will raise him up. And if he has committed sins, he will be forgiven. Confess your trespasses to one another, and pray for one another, that you may be healed. The effective, fervent prayer of a righteous man avails much. Elijah was a man with a nature like ours, and he prayed earnestly that it would not rain; and it did not rain on the land for three years and six months. And he prayed again, and the heaven gave rain, and the earth produced its fruit."

   If you are sick or suffering, what should you do?

   What type of prayer saves (heals) the sick?

   Describe the role of the church leaders (pastors) when it comes to prayer:

6. **Pray when someone else is sick or suffering—Acts 28:8.**
   "And it happened that the father of Publius lay sick of a fever and dysentery. Paul went in to him and prayed, and he laid his hands on him and healed him."

   What can you do when someone else is sick?

   What happens to Publius?

7. **Pray when you are afraid—Psalm 56:3 KJV.**
   "What time I am afraid, I will put my trust in thee."

   What should you do when you are afraid?

134

How can you put your trust in God?

8. **Pray when looking for a successor—Numbers 27:15-17 NLT.**
"Then Moses said to the LORD, 'O LORD, You are the God who gives breath to all creatures. Please appoint a new man as leader for the community. Give them someone who will guide them wherever they go and will lead them into battle, so the community of the LORD will not be like sheep without a shepherd.'"

How does Moses pray for his successor?

9. **Pray when you are barren or in a struggle—Genesis 25:21-23.**
"Now Isaac pleaded with the LORD for his wife, because she was barren; and the LORD granted his plea, and Rebekah his wife conceived. But the children struggled together within her; and she said, 'If all is well, why am I like this?' So she went to inquire of the LORD. And the LORD said to her: 'Two nations are in your womb, two peoples shall be separated from your body; One people shall be stronger than the other, And the older shall serve the younger.'"

What does Isaac do when they face barrenness?

What does the Lord do in response?

What does Rebekah do when she faces an internal struggle?

What does the Lord do in response?

Notice the two ways prayer is described in this passage: Isaac "pleaded" with the Lord in prayer, and Rebekah "inquired" of the Lord. Have you prayed in both of those ways?

10. **Pray when you face a battle and need a strategy—Judges 20:18.**
"Then the children of Israel arose and went up to the house of God to inquire of God. They said, 'Which of us shall go up first to battle against the children of Benjamin?' The LORD said, 'Judah first!'"

What should you do when you face a battle, have enemies, or need a strategy from God?

What do you think would have happened if the children of Israel had not "inquired of God" first?

11. **Pray when you need personal revival—Psalm 119.**

    Verse 25   *"My soul clings to the dust; Revive me according to Your word."*

    Verse 37   *"Turn away my eyes from looking at worthless things, and revive me in Your way."*

    Verse 40   *"Behold, I long for Your precepts; Revive me in Your righteousness."*

    Verse 88:   *"Revive me according to Your lovingkindness, So that I may keep the testimony of Your mouth."*

    Verse 107   *"I am afflicted very much; Revive me, O LORD, according to Your word."*

    Verse 149   *"Hear my voice according to Your lovingkindness; O LORD, revive me according to Your justice."*

    Verse 154   *"Plead my cause and redeem me; Revive me according to Your word."*

    Verse 156   *"Great are Your tender mercies, O LORD; Revive me according to Your judgments."*

    Verse 159   *"Consider how I love Your precepts; Revive me, O LORD, according to Your lovingkindness."*

What should you do when you need a personal revival?

12. **Pray when your land needs revival—2 Chronicles 7:14.**
"If My people who are called by My name will humble themselves, and pray and seek My face, and turn from their wicked ways, then I will hear from heaven, and will forgive their sin and heal their land."

Who is supposed to pray for their land?

What attitude should you have in prayer?

What will the Lord do?

13. **Pray when you stand against the devil—Ephesians 6:10-18.**
"Finally, my brethren, be strong in the Lord and in the power of His might. Put on the whole armor of God, that you may be able to stand against the wiles of the devil. For we do not wrestle against flesh and blood, but against principalities, against powers, against the rulers of the darkness of this age, against spiritual hosts of wickedness in the heavenly places. Therefore take

up the whole armor of God, that you may be able to withstand in the evil day, and having done all, to stand. Stand therefore, having girded your waist with truth, having put on the breastplate of righteousness, and having shod your feet with the preparation of the gospel of peace; above all, taking the shield of faith with which you will be able to quench all the fiery darts of the wicked one. And take the helmet of salvation, and the sword of the Spirit, which is the word of God; praying always with all prayer and supplication in the Spirit, being watchful to this end with all perseverance and supplication for all the saints."

According to these verses, what kind of spiritual reality are you engaged in?

Describe the spiritual armor God has given you.

In addition to putting on your spiritual armor (both offensive and defensive pieces), what should you do to stand against the wiles of the enemy?

REVELATION DROP: As a family, whenever we traveled—to school, on a road trip, or by train, plane, or boat—we prayed for God's wisdom and His protection: *"Thank You, Lord, the name of Jesus, the blood of Jesus, and the angels of God surround us and protect us. We thank You for your wisdom and protection front to back, side to side, and top to bottom—spirit, soul, and body. We believe it. In Jesus' name, amen."* Take your stand and pray God's Word over your life and family.

14. **Pray when you have a loud cry inside—Hebrews 5:7.**
"Who, in the days of His flesh, when He had offered up prayers and supplications, with vehement cries and tears to Him who was able to save Him from death, and was heard because of His godly fear."

How did Jesus pray when He was on the earth?

15. **Pray when you are thankful—Psalm 92:1.**
"It is good to give thanks to the Lord, to sing praises to Your name, O Most High."

What should you do when you are thankful?

16. **Pray when you don't feel thankful—Hebrews 13:15 ESV.**
"Through Him then let us continually offer up a sacrifice of praise to God, that is, the fruit of lips that acknowledge His name."

What do you need to do continually, even when you don't feel like it?

There are so many opportunities for prayer. Don't get locked in a box thinking you can only pray one way or at one time. God wants to hear from you at all times!

E. PRAY FOR A MOMENT OR FOR AN HOUR

We can pray for a moment, for an hour, or for longer! The Apostle Paul was known for his *make mention* style of prayer. Jesus let us know about the power of praying for *one hour*. Let's look at both.

1. **Romans 1:9**
   "For God is my witness, whom I serve with my spirit in the gospel of His Son, that without ceasing I make mention of you always in my prayers."

   How long were the Apostle Paul's prayers for those in Rome?

   REVELATION DROP: Sometimes we feel as though we need to spend a lot of time in prayer for our prayers to be effective, but the truth is we can "make mention" of people throughout the day to lift them and their needs up before the Lord.

2. **Matthew 26:36-43**
   "Then Jesus came with them to a place called Gethsemane, and said to the disciples, 'Sit here while I go and pray over there.' And He took with Him Peter and the two sons of Zebedee, and He began to be sorrowful and deeply distressed. Then He said to them, 'My soul is exceedingly sorrowful, even to death. Stay here and watch with Me.' He went a little farther and fell on His face, and prayed, saying, 'O My Father, if it is possible, let this cup pass from Me; nevertheless, not as I will, but as You will.' Then He came to the disciples and found them sleeping, and said to Peter, 'What! Could you not watch with Me one hour? Watch and pray, lest you enter into temptation. The spirit indeed is willing, but the flesh is weak.' Again, a second time, He went away and prayed, saying, 'O My Father, if this cup cannot pass away from Me unless I drink it, Your will be done.' And He came and found them asleep again, for their eyes were heavy."

   How long does Jesus want Peter to spend in prayer with Him?

   Have you ever prayed for an hour? Using The Lord's Prayer as your prayer template is a great tool for spending a productive hour with the Lord in prayer.

When can we pray? We can pray when the Spirit moves us. We can pray when the Spirit doesn't move us. We can pray when we want to. We can pray for a moment, and we can pray for an hour or longer.

F. PRAY IT OUT

What verse or passages stood out to you in this chapter? What truths stirred your heart?

Take a moment to pray and put these things into practice.

SECTION 7:

THE "WHERE" OF PRAYER

CHAPTER 15:

THE "WHERE" OF PRAYER

"The only time my prayers are never answered is on the golf course."
Billy Graham

So far, we've learned a few basics on the "what, who, why, how and when" of prayer. Now let's wrap up by looking at "where" to pray.

Is there a specified place from which we should pray? Do we need to be standing? Kneeling? Lying down? Facing east? In a closet? In church? Should we pray from our head? Heart? Let's look at all of the places from which we pray.

A. PRAY FROM THE PLACE OF YOUR HEART

We have covered a lot of ground in our study of prayer and I believe your prayer toolbox is full of tools to help you pray more effectively and with greater joy! Don't be overwhelmed by all that we have covered; but rather, trust the Holy Spirit to lead you in prayer and you'll know what prayer tools to use and when to use them. As we wrap up our study in *Getting a Grip on the Basics of Prayer*, let's revisit the truth that effective pray comes from the heart.

1. **Pray earnestly from your heart—James 5:16 AMPC.**
    "The earnest (heartfelt, continued) prayer of a righteous man makes tremendous power available [dynamic in its working]."

    What type of prayer makes power available?

    What does "earnest prayer" mean to you?

    What does "heartfelt prayer" mean to you?

    What does "continued prayer" mean to you?

    REVELATION DROP: What does it mean to pray "earnest, heartfelt" prayers? We drove by a cute little country church with this quote on their church sign: *"Pray like you are the third monkey trying to get on Noah's Ark."* Although humorous, that's a good picture of earnest, heartfelt prayer!

2. **Pour out your heart to Him—Psalm 62:8.**

"Trust in Him at all times, you people; pour out your heart before Him; God is a refuge for us."

How would you describe the idea of "pouring out your heart" to the Lord?

3. **Pray from a clear heart—Proverbs 4:23.**

"Keep your heart with all diligence, for out of it spring the issues of life."

How are we to guard our hearts?

What flows out of your heart?

REVELATION DROP: Everything in our lives and in our relationship with the Lord begins in our hearts (our spirit). Our heart is the central part of us. It's our personal headquarters. God doesn't want us to allow anything to hinder our hearts—fear, doubt, busyness, hatred, anger, strife, or any other troublesome thing. In addition, the Lord wants our heart to stay clear and free from condemnation. That's because our heart is the place from which we communicate with God, and it's the place He speaks to within us. No wonder God told us to guard it!

4. **Pray from a heart full of faith and love—1 John 3:18-22.**

"My little children, let us not love in word or in tongue, but in deed and in truth. And by this we know that we are of the truth, and shall assure our hearts before Him. For if our heart condemns us, God is greater than our heart, and knows all things. Beloved, if our heart does not condemn us, we have confidence toward God. And whatever we ask we receive from Him, because we keep His commandments and do those things that are pleasing in His sight."

What gives you assurance and confidence before God?

If your heart does not condemn you, what can you be certain of when you ask?

REVELATION DROP: If there is anyone or anything that is causing your heart to feel condemned, why not take a few moments to clear that up before the Lord. Years ago, a friend of mine told me a story about a woman he knew who was trying to get pregnant. This woman and her husband had been believing God for years to have a baby, but each month the pregnancy test came up negative. She was so discouraged she decided to spend some extra time in prayer seeking the Lord and asking for His help. As she did, the Lord spoke to her heart in a gentle way letting her know she needed to forgive her grandfather. Her grandfather had long since died, but when he was alive, he had sexually abused her when she was little. She had never told anyone, and yet unforgiveness was resident in her heart.

She gathered her courage and met with her family. She told them what had transpired, and she also told them that from that day on she was choosing to forgive her grandfather and move on with her life. This took courage and obedience on her part and as a result, her family rallied around her with love and support. The "happily ever after" part is that several weeks later, she found out she was pregnant!

If you have struggled to get answers to prayer you know God has promised you, perhaps this is a good time to spend extra time seeking the Lord and asking for His help, just as she did. Of course, your story may be different than hers, but God will meet you with heartfelt answers just as He did for her.

B.   PRAY FROM THE PLACE OF YOUR AUTHORITY IN CHRIST

Our authority to pray comes from Jesus and His finished work on the cross. Through His life, death, burial, resurrection, and being seated in heavenly places; we, too, have been buried with Him, raised from the dead, and seated with Him. He has raised us up together with Him to sit together with Him in those heavenly places (Ephesians 1:20; 2:6).

What a gift! The moment we received Jesus as our Lord, He placed us "in Him" and seated us with Christ. far above all principalities and powers. He's given us a seat with Jesus, and He's given us the authority to use His name. Let's look at this.

1.   **Pray from your seated position—Ephesians 2:4-6.**
"But God, who is rich in mercy, because of His great love with which He loved us, even when we were dead in trespasses, made us alive together with Christ (by grace you have been saved), and raised us up together, and made us sit together in the heavenly places in Christ Jesus."

How does God feel about you?

Where has God raised and seated you?

REVELATION DROP: I love the way Ephesians 2:6 puts it from these three translations.

>> *"And he raised us up together with Him and made us sit down together [giving us joint seating with Him] in the heavenly sphere [by virtue of our being] in Christ Jesus (the Messiah, the Anointed One)."* AMPC

>> *"He raised us up with Christ, the exalted One. And we ascended with Him into the glorious perfection and authority of the heavenly realm for we are now co-seated as one with Christ."* TPT

>> *"And did raise [us] up together and did seat [us] together in the heavenly [places] in Christ Jesus."* YLT

Just as sure as Jesus was raised from the dead and seated far above every principality, every power, every name, and everything that could be named on earth and under the earth; we, too, have been raised up and seated far above all of those very same things because we are in Christ, co-seated with Him. When we understand what Christ has done for us, we can pray powerful, productive prayers from our position of being seated with Christ in heavenly places.

2. **Pray from being seated far above—Ephesians 1:20-22.**
"Which He worked in Christ when He raised Him from the dead and seated Him at His right hand in the heavenly places, far above all principality and power and might and dominion, and every name that is named, not only in this age but also in that which is to come. And He put all things under His feet, and gave Him to be head over all things to the church."

Where is Jesus seated?

What is under His feet?

What is He the head of?

Since you are seated together with Christ, where does that put you?

REVELATION DROP: When we pray, remember we are not praying from an "earthly" position looking up; we are praying from our "heavenly" position—looking down. We are actually seated with Christ in heavenly places, far above all principalities, powers, might, dominion, and every name that can be named.

It doesn't matter how crazy, ungodly, or anti-Christ this world gets; we can always pray from our position of victory in Christ! We don't pray prayers of unbelief or hopelessness filled with fear or anger. We are not begging God to do something; we're simply asking for and appropriating what He's already provided. We don't pray from defeat. We pray from victory. We're enforcing the defeat of the enemy that Jesus has already accomplished. This is not a position of striving, weakness, anxiety, or fear; rather it is a prayer position of faith, boldness, and power in Christ.

When we pray from our place of authority in Christ, we pray prayers of confidence, prayers based on the finished work of what Jesus has done through the cross. When we pray from this place of authority, we pray, we say, we decree, we declare according to God's Word, which is His will. And when we do that, God, His angelic realm, and all of heaven goes to work answering our prayers and fulfilling His will.

This reality gives us a huge supernatural advantage in prayer, and every Christian can step into it with boldness. Maybe you feel like the most unspiritual person in the whole world and think, *"Oh, all those other super-spiritual people can pray like that with all that authority but not me. I can't pray like that"*; that's not true! You can pray with the same authority as Christ. You are in His body and seated in heavenly places. Even if you feel like you are the skin on the bottom of the little toe in the Body of Christ, you are still in the Body of Christ; and you still have been raised up far above every authority and every name that can be named. Don't let intimidation, a low self-esteem, or negative thoughts talk you out of praying bold prayers.

In the name of Jesus, rise up and take your place seated with Christ!

Let's not squander this wonderful privilege; let's pray! (If this topic is new to you, one of the best books on this subject is the classic, *The Believers Authority* by Kenneth E. Hagin.)

C. PRAY FROM ANY PLACE

We can pray anywhere—in public and in private! You can pray on a mountain, in a boat, through the desert, walking in a valley, on an airplane, or while scuba diving. We can pray anywhere! Let's look at a few more locations the Bible mentions.

1. **Pray in your room—Matthew 6:6.**
    "But you, when you pray, go into your room, and when you have shut your door, pray to your Father who is in the secret place; and your Father who sees in secret will reward you openly."

    Where should you pray?

    Where is your "secret place"?

    REVELATION DROP: In different seasons of our lives, I have enjoyed various locations for prayer. Most often, I like to create my own private prayer room by kneeling by our sofa with a blanket wrapped around my head and shoulders. I also enjoy going for a prayer drive in my car. I like to drive along the backroads or around the perimeter of our county to pray for our city and our church. At times, I like to lay with my face on the floor as I pray and seek the Lord in prayer and worship. At other times, I like to walk and pray. Do you have a special place to pray? Perhaps it's your prayer room, bedroom, or closet? Your Father sees you no matter where your place of prayer happens to be.

2. **Pray in a storm from a fish's belly—Jonah 2:1-2.**
    "Then Jonah prayed to the LORD his God from the fish's belly. And he said: "I cried out to the LORD because of my affliction, and He answered me.""

    From where does Jonah pray?

    What does God do?

    You may not be in a fish's belly, but you may feel as though you are underwater in the middle of a storm and afflicted. You can pray from there!

3. **Pray in the valley—Psalm 23:4-6.**
    "Yea, though I walk through the valley of the shadow of death, I will fear no evil; for You are with me; Your rod and Your staff, they comfort me. You prepare a table before me in the presence of my enemies; You anoint my head with oil; my cup runs over. Surely goodness and mercy shall

145

follow me all the days of my life; and I will dwell in the house of the LORD."

When you walk through difficult valleys, what can you pray?

4. **Pray in church—Matthew 21:13.**
   "He said to them, 'It is written, "My house shall be called a house of prayer."'"

What does Jesus call His house?

What should we do there?

D. PRAY FROM YOUR PLACE OF QUIETNESS AND REST

In prayer, it's good to quiet your heart before the Lord and pray from the place of rest in Christ.

1. **Psalm 46:10**
   "Be still, and know that I am God; I will be exalted among the nations, I will be exalted in the earth!"

What type of disposition does God want us to have?

2. **Isaiah 40:31**
   "But those who wait on the LORD shall renew their strength; they shall mount up with wings like eagles, they shall run and not be weary, they shall walk and not faint."

How do you "wait on the Lord" in prayer?

What happens for those who "wait on the Lord"?

REVELATION DROP: We experience mental, emotional, and spiritual rest when we turn off the noise and wait on the Lord. Often, it takes us a bit of effort to get quiet and still. We have to turn off the distractions that try to get our attention. It may be the sudden need to make a checklist of all the things we need to do for the next year, or a sudden urge to do a massive spring cleaning of our home. Other big distractions are odd random desires—a desire to check sport scores, organize our refrigerator, or make ourselves a bowl of ice cream. These things distract us from the Lord. Maybe we have the television or music playing, and we find ourselves distracted with a program or song lyrics.

Another big distraction to our prayer time and waiting on the Lord is our phone. Most of us have our mobile phones with us 24/7, so it's easy to grab our phones to check our social media or text messages right in the middle of our prayer time with the Lord. The Lord would like our undivided attention and an opportunity to talk with us. Have you ever been out to dinner with people who were constantly checking their phones? How did that make you feel? I'll never forget an interview we were conducting for a young adult, and in the middle of the interview, he checked his phone several times. He was distracted and not focused on the interview!

Let's spend undistracted time with the Lord to talk to Him and more importantly to hear His voice. In doing so, we'll experience His rest and strength.

3. **Zephaniah 3:17**

   "The LORD your God in your midst, the Mighty One, will save; He will rejoice over you with gladness, He will quiet you with His love, He will rejoice over you with singing."

   Not only do you sing and pray to the Lord, but what does the Lord do over you?

E. PRAY FROM YOUR PLACE OF BEING HUNGRY FOR GOD

This is one of the best places to pray from—a heart hungry for God! The Lord has promised to answer our hunger and thirst.

1. **Matthew 5:6**

   "Blessed are those who hunger and thirst for righteousness, for they shall be filled."

   Who does God fill?

2. **Hebrews 11:6**

   "But without faith it is impossible to please Him, for he who comes to God must believe that He is, and that He is a rewarder of those who diligently seek Him."

   Who does God reward?

3. **Psalm 34:10 AMPC**

   "The young lions lack food and suffer hunger, but they who seek (inquire of and require) the Lord [by right of their need and on the authority of His Word], none of them shall lack any beneficial thing."

   What happens for those who seek the Lord?

4. **Psalm 105:1-4 AMPC**

   "O give thanks unto the Lord, call upon His name, make known His doings among the peoples! Sing to Him, sing praises to Him; meditate on and talk of all His marvelous deeds and devoutly praise them. Glory in His holy name; let the hearts of those rejoice who seek and require the Lord [as their indispensable necessity]. Seek, inquire of and for the Lord, and crave Him and His strength (His might and inflexibility to temptation); seek and require His face and His pres-

ence [continually] evermore."

According to this passage, in what ways can you communicate with the Lord?

How do you define the words seek, require, indispensable necessity, inquire, crave, and require?

5. **Psalm 27:8 AMPC**
    "You have said, Seek My face [inquire for and require My presence as your vital need]. My heart says to You, Your face (Your presence), Lord, will I seek, inquire for, and require [of necessity and on the authority of Your Word]."

What does the Lord ask you to do?

What does your heart say to the Lord?

F.   PRAY IT OUT

What verse or passages stood out to you in this chapter? What truths stirred your heart?

Take a moment to pray and put these things into practice.

THE END

CONCLUSION

"The end of a thing is better than its beginning..."
Ecclesiastes 7:8

Congratulations! You did it! You've completed *Getting a Grip on the Basics of Prayer.* I hope your heart is full of faith to pray.

>> Just think, as you pray, your heavenly Father wants to have an intimate prayer dialogue with you—enjoy this incredible blessing!

>> Just think, the Lord wants to answer your prayer requests and give good gifts to you when you ask Him—may your joy be full!

>> Just think, through prayer you can work with God to produce fruit and make an eternal difference—this is a privilege beyond measure!

May you enjoy the same blessings enjoyed by the late George Mueller who said, *"I live in the spirit of prayer. I pray as I walk about, when I lie down and when I rise up. And the answers are always coming."*

Now, it's up to you. Pray without ceasing.

Romans 12:12
"Rejoicing in hope, patient in tribulation, continuing steadfastly in prayer."

WHAT MUST YOU DO TO BE SAVED?

THE PRAYER OF SALVATION

"If you openly declare that Jesus is Lord and believe in your heart
that God raised him from the dead, you will be saved.
For it is by believing in your heart that you are made right with God,
and it is by openly declaring your faith that you are saved."
Romans 10:9-10 NLT

God loves you–no matter who you are, no matter what your past. God love you so much that He gave his one and only begotten Son for you. The Bible tells us that *"...whoever believes in him shall not perish but have eternal life"* (John 3:16 NIV). Jesus laid down His life and rose again so that we could spend eternity with Him in heaven and experience His absolute best on earth. If you would like to receive Jesus into your life, say the following prayer out loud and mean it from your heart.

Heavenly Father, I come to You admitting that I am a sinner. Right now, I choose to turn away from sin, and I ask You to cleanse me of all unrighteousness. I believe that Your Son, Jesus, died on the cross to take away my sins. I also believe that He rose again from the dead so that I might be forgiven of my sins and made righteous through faith in Him. I call upon the name of Jesus Christ to be the Savior and Lord of my life. Jesus, I choose to follow You and ask that you fill me with the power of the Holy Spirit. I declare that right now I am a child of God. I am free from sin and full of the righteousness of God. I am saved in Jesus' name. Amen.

If you prayed this prayer to receive Jesus Christ as your Savior for the first time, please contact us at: **www.thebasicswithbeth.com** to receive a free book.

ACKNOWLEGMENTS

SPECIAL THANKS

"Appreciate good people. They are hard to come by."
Unknown

For every book written, there are many people who helped to make it possible, and heaven knows each name!

I appreciate and would like to give *special thanks* to these wonderful people for their help with this book.

My heavenly Father, Jesus, and the Holy Spirit: You make everything possible. All that I am is by Your grace, and all that I do is for Your glory.

My husband, Jeff Jones: you are always the first person to read (and reread) every manuscript and the first person to encourage me along the way. Thank you for always loving and serving me so selflessly in seasons of writing–and at all other times, too!

My prayer mentors: these people may not know how much they've helped me in my prayer life (and thus this book), but they have! I appreciate and honor these people whom God has used to nurture my prayer life— Andrea Hammack, Michelle Clowe, the Campus Crusade for Christ staff at Western Michigan University and Boston College, Pastor Dave Williams, the Fire Escape prayer group, Mary Jo Fox, Rev. Kenneth E. Hagin, Pastor Ken and Lynette Hagin, Rev. Patsy Cameneti, the Rhema Bible College and Prayer School staff, and numerous prayer authors. Your teaching and example in prayer have enriched my life greatly.

My family and friends: Meghan Hock, Tara Farrell, April Wedel, Richard Pilger, Aaron Johnson, Matt Munson, Amanda Harrison, Erica Giesow and Bruce Barton. Thank you for praying, reading, proofing, and sharing your very helpful feedback on various parts of this book. Big thanks to Meghan for creating the rain cycle art and to Amanda for creating the back pages.

My editor and friends at Harrison House Publishers: Joy Abad, Brad Herman, Alex Knepper, Kaye Mountz, Ashley Mellott and Eileen Rockwell. Thank you Joy for your attention to detail and your expertise in editing. My heartfelt thanks go to Brad and the entire team at Harrison House Publishers, I greatly appreciate you, your faith and your partnership in getting this book to the world.

My family, extended family, Valley Family Church family, and the "Get a Grip on the Basics" family: you have been the primary subjects of my prayers for most of my life! I love seeing the fruit of God's goodness in your lives.

As always, I pray that God's people are encouraged and eternal fruit for His honor and glory is the result of this book.

ABOUT THE AUTHOR

BETH JONES

"I'm a writer. Anything you say or do may be used in a story."
Unknown

Beth Jones is a Bible teacher, pastor and author who has been helping people "get a grip" on the basics of God's Word for thirty years. She has written more than 20 books and her flagship book, *Getting a Grip on the Basics*, has sold more than 250,000 copies worldwide and has been translated into twenty-five other languages. Her *The Basics With Beth* television program airs on several networks internationally, including Hillsong Channel and TBN Nejat in the Middle East.

Beth and her husband, Jeff, founded Valley Family Church in Kalamazoo, Michigan, in 1991, where she often speaks and where they still serve there as senior pastors. She is a podcast host and teaches thousands online through her Basics University. Beth and Jeff have four grown children and four grandchildren (and counting!) and live in Kalamazoo.

Connect with Beth at, *thebasicswithbeth.com*

THE BASICS UNIVERSITY ONLINE
by beth jones

Customize your spiritual growth, develop unshakeable faith and deepen your relationship with the Lord through our online, basics video courses! Beth will take you by the hand as you dig into the Bible, scripture-by-scripture, to get the basics together!

Sign up for your first course today at thebasicsuniversity.com.

WATCH & LISTEN
TO THE BIBLE BASICS
from beth jones

The more of God's Word you hear, watch, study and read, the more faith will come and fill your heart. Beth Jones has loads of free Bible teaching available on The Basics With Beth Podcast, YouTube Channel, Rumble and Smart TV Channels. You can also catch her television program weekly on the Hillsong Channel.

Discover ways to watch and listen at
thebasicswithbeth.com.